Leaving the Military™:

Your Deployment Guide to Corporate America

By Marcea A. Weiss

Darryl,

Thanks for all of your advice & help "transitioning!"

Marcea

Advance Praise

Leaving the Military™ is like having a trusted friend and adviser to help you make the transition from the military to corporate America. It's a no-nonsense, pragmatic guide to preparing for and implementing a career development plan. Having the tools at your fingertips along with a step-by-step plan that breaks a big rock into smaller chunks is especially helpful. The competency models Marcea has shared are in sync with what hiring managers are looking for today. Being able to translate your military experiences into the language of business will go a long way toward making your transition a success. *Leaving the Military™* provides the resources you need so that there are no excuses about being too busy to dedicate a few minutes each week to working on your plan!

Darryl Carson
Manager of Learning and Development
at Synaptics, California

Leaving the Military™ provides a systematic recipe for success! It is a "must read" for those planning to move out from a military career into the civilian sector, especially in today's economic times. Marcea's book is highly recommended reading for all pay grades and specialty fields. With its personal insights, recommendations and checklists, it guides you in the development of a course of action and mindset to achieve a highly successful career change!

John J. Marks, Captain
USCGR, experienced military transitioner from
enlisted, officer, active duty and reserve positions
over 37 years of active and reserve military service.

There are countless workbooks and seminars for transitioning veterans to utilize in preparation for the next step. *Leaving the Military*™ is the "king of the hill" when it comes to unwrapping your military experience and exposing those tangible skills that corporate America is looking for day after day. Military training produces high quality skilled personnel who will become anchor employees and business leaders. Marcea will show you how to Leverage your strengths, Develop you weaknesses! Leaving the Military is your go to guide to assist you and your family the next successful chapter in your life.

Joseph R. Grossi, United States Navy, 21 years, Retired.

Leaving the Military™

Your Deployment Guide to Corporate America

By Marcea A. Weiss

Calypso Publishing

Contents

Appendices

Foreword

By

Kelly Perdew

Second Season Winner

on "The Apprentice"

When Donald Trump said to me, "You're hired," in the finale of season two of "The Apprentice," I credited much of my success to one thing — my U.S. military training. I had embarked upon one of many transitions that I would make during my life.

The career transition from the military to corporate America is undeniably challenging. You are leaving a very tight-knit team and well-defined working culture. I'll share the advice with you here that I share with all of my military brothers and sisters as they look to transition. Be confident! Be confident because you have the leadership skills that are needed to be successful. Be confident of what you've accomplished in your past. There aren't many people in the private sector who have done as much as you have in the military.

The military exposed you to many types of work environments with many different types of people. You learned how to deliver results or get the mission done while being flexible. Flexibility is an understated quality, for, in the end, the winner is the one with the most options. Flexibility was something that helped me to be successful during the Apprentice competition.

On one episode, we were tasked with a fashion show. In the end, I inspired four outfits for our team. People thought it was strange to see me, a military veteran, designing apparel, but this is the type of flexibility that is enabled by growing up in the military. You learn how to problem-solve and how to do what is needed to be successful!

Now that you are confident and feeling good, it is time to get to work! It's time to map out your transition plan and start taking action to make it a reality.

When separating from the military, you have to be introspective — to examine your personal goals in order to reach them. Just as you would in the military, treat your transition to corporate America as you would treat a new mission.

Get started by learning about the business sector and the lingo of corporate America. You can't fall back on military-speak when you are talking to the human resources or hiring department. Learn the language of business and about the new environment that will be your new home.

Passion is a key principle. It will play a crucial role during your transition and hiring timeline. It is important to know what you are excited about — now and in the future — and then share that excitement with the hiring manager and team. When you really have passion for what you are doing, it impacts your success in so many different ways. Certainly the people that you work with feel it. Your customers, your colleagues and your associates will notice. You're happier, and everyone around you is happier.

Networking is also vital. Use and develop your networks. Many people in business leadership positions have served in the military. Do your homework on organizations headed up by those who have served or organizations that have hired from the military. This can help to ease the pressure of your transition as you are able to interview with and join an organization that will better understand you and will value your skill and contributions from the start. Your strong sense of selflessness, duty and passion will set you above the rest in accomplishing the goals of your team, your department and your company.

As you look to your future in corporate America, work to identify your primary objectives and the intermediate objectives that lead up to them. Don't do this in isolation. Network. Build a team. Get help in making a successful plan. "Fail to plan, plan to fail." It's really that simple. Personally, professionally, financially, you name it — you need a plan to find success.

Broadly speaking, success is knowing that you have done everything possible to maximize the opportunities for you and your loved ones. It means knowing you worked hard, you made good decisions based on the best information you could acquire, and that you thought about how your decisions would impact the people closest to you, both immediately and in the future.

I applaud you for seeking out the information that will help you to find success. Be informed. Be prepared. Be successful! Marcea's *Leaving the*

Leaving the Military™

Military™ and interactive transition process will help you to find the right path. Take advantage of all of the information, examples and exercises included in these pages.

> *Good luck on your journey!*
> Kelly Perdew

About Kelley Perdew:

Kelly Perdew graduated from the United States Military Academy, West Point, the Anderson School of Management at UCLA, and the UCLA School of Law. He served as a military intelligence officer, successfully completing Airborne and Ranger school, in the U.S. Army and held multiple chairman and CEO positions before winning the second season of "The Apprentice."

Kelly outlined his lessons learned at West Point and during his subsequent military service centered on ten essential principles for effective leadership. Kelly documented these skills in *Take Command: 10 Leadership Principles I Learned in the Military and Put to Work for Donald Trump* (Regnery Publishing, 2006). They are: duty, impeccability, passion, perseverance, planning, teamwork, loyalty, flexibility, selfless service and integrity.

Kelly Perdew can be reached through his website at www.kellyperdew.com.

Introduction

* * * * * * * * * * * * * * *

A Success Story

During the phone interview, I could tell that Jack was a bit nervous, but, overall he seemed excited. He moved rather smoothly through the questions that I posed. We went through many of the usual questions that I was in the routine of asking, such as:

"Tell me about yourself"

"Tell me about a specific project that you worked on or led. What steps did you take to overcome adversity and to deliver results?"

"Why are you interested in our company/this role?"

His answers were pretty straightforward. Jack had specific examples prepared from his time in the military. In a few instances, he fell back on his military jargon and acronyms, but easily responded when I asked for clarification. That was important because I knew that if Jack was invited to an onsite interview, he would have to be able to speak in a way that our non-military-experienced team members would understand.

As we talked through the 45-minute phone session, Jack let me know that he was considering a number of options, but that our opportunity was particularly exciting to him as he was hoping to get back in the tech sector in a role that offered a development path into leadership. This showed me that he had spent some time reading the job description and information that I had sent a few days prior and I appreciated that.

Jack also seemed excited about our opportunity. I could tell because I could almost hear him smile and sit up straight — even lean forward in his seat — during the phone interview. He also asked some very insightful questions about the opportunity which again showed me that he had prepared and was truly interested.

When the phone interview was complete and I sat for a few moments to consider my recommendation and his results, a few things came to mind. I thought about what he had told me in the conversation and his responses to my questions and tried to summarize his fit (or lack of) for the role.

My mind naturally went back to the points in the interview where Jack seemed excited, to the examples and responses where I noticed he had "perked up." These were the areas that I knew he had true interest and which were usually related to a very proud accomplishment and something that he cared deeply about.

I reviewed the competency model that historically determines success for this role: problem-solving, autonomy, customer-focus and ability to persevere. I thought about the example that he had shared with me about leading his maintenance team to find the necessary parts and to complete the vehicle repairs for their customer units. These units were very dependent on their vehicles to be able to successfully complete their mission.

Jack had described how his team was short one team member, how parts were scarce and how it was critical to their customer unit that they completed this repair as soon as possible. Jack took steps to get his group together and talked them through the plan. He described how he got them involved in the problem-solving and execution to successfully find the parts and complete the repair. In the end, Jack and his team were recognized for their efforts as they went "above and beyond" the normal procedure to satisfy or exceed their customer units' needs in 12 fewer hours than expected.

I could really see how the actions that Jack took in this military environment would translate well in our corporation. Like any organization, we could never have too many leaders and we were continuously being asked to do more with less. Our customers depended on our services and timely response or would quickly move to our competitors' solutions. Based on the specific examples that Jack described in the phone interview, I could see him in our team today, working well with the group, motivating them to do more, increasing customer satisfaction and delivering results.

It concerned me that Jack would be entering our marketing organization without any prior experience in this area, but I had seen from past successful military-experienced hires in our organization that the right military candidate can overcome this lack of experience by using the skills gained in the military —

confidence, leadership and persistence — to develop more quickly.

In the end, it was not a difficult decision to make. I invited Jack onsite over

the next two weeks for a full day of interviews with our hiring team. He would

spend the day talking with peers, subordinates and leaders in our organization to

learn more about our opportunity and our company and to prove his "fit." I was

really excited to see how he would fare onsite and found myself hoping that he

would take advantage of the available time leading up to the interview to further

polish his skills and to learn more about our organization. I was hoping to see

Jack shine!

* * * * * * * * * * * * * * *

How did Jack prepare for this interview? How did he ensure his success?

How will you? As one of the more than 400,000 active duty and part-time

military members transitioning from the military this year, you may not know

where to start. As an experienced leader, you have spent much of your life

surrounded by the military culture and environment.

With current world conflicts and regular deployments, you may have had

limited time to prepare for this transition or to explore the vast number of

opportunities available to you. Whether you are leaving in the next few weeks or

months or considering it in the upcoming years, you have a lot of questions that need answering. Sure, it would be great to spend multiple years planning this new and uncharted course, but that is not always realistic. You need one consolidated source that can map out this path logically, and with focus. You need a clearly outlined process to harness and communicate your strengths and to help you determine how to best match them to available positions. You need a guide that will engage you in a manner familiar to the aggressive military training of your past. You want a guide that will not waste your time with a lot of "fluffy" theories, but one that will get "down to business" and teach you what you need to know in the military-friendly BLUF (bottom line up front) format.

You want a guide that will teach you what you need to know!

This book is that guide. By mapping out a chronological, no-nonsense path that ends with you successfully assuming a leadership role in your new position in corporate America, this guide fills a currently unmet need to:

- ○ Streamline the preparation process in seven to-the-point checklist style chapters that can be adapted to individual needs.

- ○ Maintain focus on being successful with the one key relationship that drives transition success: the relationship between the military candidate and the hiring team and hiring manager, i.e., where the "rubber meets the road."

- ○ Present an unbiased view of options available to military candidates, facilitating the right and best decision for you and for your family.

- o Include interactive, workbook-style activities to increase self-awareness and understanding, which are critical to the interview process and critical to delivering results in your future role.

- o Outline a path to avoid common mistakes military leaders make when interviewing and transitioning.

- o Encourage you to consider all of the benefits of a career in the military and in corporate America to make the best-informed decision for you and your family.

A transition is a challenging and stressful time for you and your family as you look for a trustworthy source of information and a clear explanation of your options. Many organizations want to help, but what is their angle? Who are they really trying to help? With limited time available, where can you get the highest return on your time invested? With this book, you will be able to clearly and objectively think through and prepare for important areas such as:

- o **Planning**: Is this decision right for me? What is the right path and direction? What will make me happy? What is the right timeline for me and how can I be sure to stay on course?

- o **Communicating**: How do I match my experience with the skill required in the new position? What experience will America value? How do I communicate my experience effectively?

- o **Standing Out**: How does corporate America view the military? What do they expect from me? How can I excel and stand out from the start?

- **Sequencing**: How do I get started in making a successful career transition from the military? What are the most important steps in this process? What should I do first?

- **Networking**: Who can I talk to for advice during this process? How should I reach them?

- **Understanding Hiring Managers**: Who are they and when will I meet them? What is important to them? What are common errors that I can avoid?

- **Planning for Success**: What can I do to rise above the competition and not just be a "good" candidate but prepare to be a "great" candidate?

- **Partnering**: What is the benefit of Military Recruiters, what types of models exist, and which one, if any, is the right one for me?

You can be sure that corporate America values the experience that you bring with you. Successful Fortune 500 companies have led the way with established military hiring programs. General Electric, Home Depot, Johnson Controls, Coca-Cola, Sprint and Lockheed Martin are a few examples of military-friendly companies as recently ranked by *GI Jobs* Magazine.

A current Google™ search shows that no less than 20 (for profit) recruiting groups are currently looking to help military leaders make a successful transition to corporate America. That is sure proof of the demand that exists! With the expected retirement timeline of the baby boomer generation over the next few years and with the increased military media coverage through the war in Iraq, this demand is on the rise.

Corporate America wants to hire you, and many organizations want to help you to transition, but who should you trust and what steps should you take first?

This book will help you to bring all of these sources together to determine the right path for you.

With more than nine years in the Army as a Blackhawk Helicopter Test Pilot, Maintenance Manager, Training Officer and more, I stood where you are standing now, preparing for the unknown. After my transition, I was offered a unique and valuable perspective as a hiring and development manager in corporate America working with new military hires as well as new college graduates. I observed the process from both ends and have applied my process improvement skills acquired throughout my working career, and as a certified Lean Six Sigma Black Belt, to deliver these streamlined steps to you. Take these steps, practice them (and then practice them some more) and apply them to accelerate your successful path to corporate America! These are the things that I wished someone had told me before I began my transitional journey over ten years ago.

Open the pages to prepare for and tackle the remarkable opportunities awaiting you in corporate America!

How to Use *Leaving the Military*™:
As Your "Weapon" to
Accelerate Your Path To Corporate America!

Process Overview

The *Leaving the Military*™ transition process is summarized with a visual timeline to help you keep your progress on track (see next page). The process works its way up the stairway from the lower left to the top right and allows you to plot your milestones across the lower horizontal axis. As you progress from "external" to "internal" to "interview" and to "path," you will better understand your objective and yourself, while refining your timeline for success.

Each step builds upon the other, allowing you to refine your plan and your timeline as you go along. The strategy starts with the bottom left-hand corner by better understanding corporate America and by determining your initial desired destination. The percentage values below each colored step describe how much of your overall transition timeline should be allotted to each area. This makes the *Leaving the Military*™ transition process fully adjustable for each individual timeline.

The vertical Y axis represents increased refinement of transition skills and your progress towards transition preparation. The horizontal X axis represents the time available from your transition start until the day of your first planned interview.

Leaving the Military™ Transition Strategy

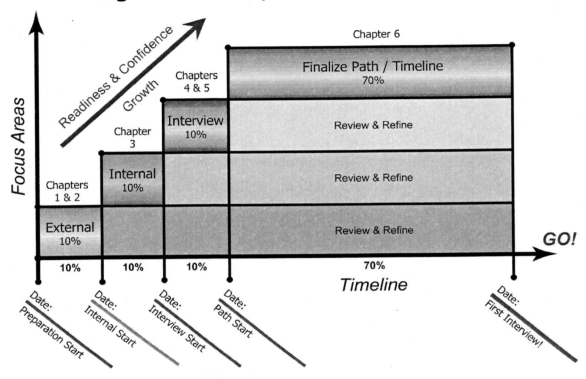

You will notice that the first three blocks, External, Internal and Interview,

are each allotted 10% of your available preparation time, while the last Path

block on the top right is allotted 70% of the overall timeline. The short burst of

10% effort allocated to the first three blocks will help you to build your detailed

timeline in chapter six. You will also notice that once you complete each of the

first three blocks, your effort for each area is not complete. You are encouraged

to continue your development in that area as you take on the next topic area or block. The topic areas, therefore, build upon each other as you work toward your transition date.

Let's look at a brief summary of what's involved in each of the steps.

External: Chapters 1 and 2 are included in the initial "External" block and generally leave you with a better understanding of what it's like in corporate America to better plan the desired destination of your transitional path. Chapter One focuses on gaining a better understanding of corporate America and what's available to you as a transitioning military leader. You will also determine your initial direction and high level objectives for your future career. Chapter Two discusses the concept of customer focus. Learn what "customer focus" means and, that, "Oh, by the way," you've been doing it for most of your military life, at least on the good days!

Internal: Chapter Three is included in the "Internal" block and will provide an opportunity to focus internally to better understand yourself. The chapter focus is to spend time reflecting on yourself and to ask those around you to help you to learn more about yourself. You will identify your strengths and weaknesses and competency profile. This profile will allow you to determine what to do today to focus your improvement in the direction of your career goals and to prepare to match your profile with positions in corporate America.

Interview and Preparation: Chapters Four and Five are included in the "Interview" block and generally describe the preparation needed to allow you to communicate your fit and goals. You will build your action plan and path. You will now refine your original timeline, adding greater details and using your project management skills to keep your progress on course, as you complete your resume, improve your interviewing skills and prepare your interview wardrobe. This will be fun, but not easy, as we will look at mistakes many military-experienced candidates make during an interview and during their transition. (Names will be removed to protect the not-so-innocent!)

Finalize Path and Timeline: Chapter Six is included in the "Finalize Path and Timeline" block and generally describes how you will work to refine and stick to your plan and schedule. Many recruiting partnership agreements exist and we will explore them to find out which option works the best for your personal transition strategy. We will put the finishing touches on your interview preparation and look at what happens after the interviews to prepare you for negotiation and final decision-making on available positions.

Go!: Chapter Seven is included in the "Go!" section and generally describes what you'll need to do to deliver or (better yet) to *exceed* the results that you've promised during the interview phase. We'll use the *Leaving the Military*™ Kick Start Strategy to help you to plan for the adjustment. We will look at effective ways to be sure that you will "hit the ground running" in your new role and explore some important pointers on how to effectively approach this important time of your life.

Get Started! Each chapter ends with an interactive workbook-style section drawing out your participation and allowing you to effectively fight off the enemy — procrastination! Specific questions are asked with room for your written responses to guide your progress and to ensure your participation. Be sure to use this book as it is designed, as an interactive workbook. Write in it. Scribble. Highlight. Use it!

Now let's get started!

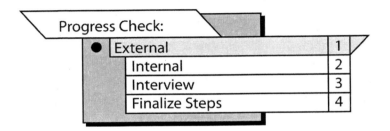

Progress Check:		
● External		1
Internal		2
Interview		3
Finalize Steps		4

Chapter One (External)

Evaluate the opportunity.

OK, let's get started! We've got a lot to do, but, realistically, is it more than what is involved in a real-world or training center deployment? No! So, be confident that you'll have what it takes and that you will be successful!

Let's start with your timeline. Be conservative with your planning. You may not have all of the variables worked out, but set up the most likely, most conservative timeline combination and assign dates on your *Leaving the Military™* Transition Strategy timeline on page 13. You will continue to update these values as you go along, but, for now, let's set an initial timeline.

Start with your end goal in mind. Think about and visualize your successful transition timeline. When are you likely to be able to schedule your first interview — over the phone or onsite? For most people, this process will start when you are able to take leave (PCS or terminal or other) to be able to conduct a phone interview or to go to the employer's location for an onsite interview. Note: onsite interviews are usually preceded by one or many telephone interviews, after which the employer may invite you onsite for an in-person interview. Most employers are looking for you to start within a month or so of your successful onsite interview, build that into your transitional plan.

You may now be very early in your decision process. In fact, you may still be working to determine the correct path to take, including remaining in the military. Or you may be reaching your military retirement timeline.

If you are deciding whether or not to transition prior to your 20-year retirement, keep a couple of things in mind as you decide when or if you should talk with your leadership team. Honest and open communication is important, but don't be too eager in announcing your plans to transition, at least until you've made up your mind. There are a couple of reasons for this and they will make more sense as you consider the situation from your leadership team's perspective.

First of all, as genuinely concerned as your chain of command is for your wellbeing, as soon as you announce your intentions, they are likely to see you in a different light. From their point of view and for that of the team, it does not make sense to invest a lot of training or other money into someone who will be leaving soon. From the perspective of the unit and of the military, it makes more sense to invest the money into someone who will be around to contribute to the mission. So keep this in mind before you make any grand announcements.

Secondly, as you learn more about corporate America and some of its highs and lows, you may decide that this is not for you. (See the Appendix B for a discussion of some reasons why it actually may make more sense for you to stay in the military.) It is a much easier conversation to have with your chain of command once you've made up your mind than to sound as if you are uncertain in your choices.

By the way, be prepared for the conversation to go on with your leadership team for some time after you tell them of your plans. If you've been the type of over-achiever who is usually able to plan ahead and make a successful transition, then you probably have a great track record from your military career and are someone who they don't want to see leave the military service. In that case, it is only natural that they will encourage you to stay and will put some effort and thought into your retention.

Once you've thought through your options clearly, you can have a great conversation with your leadership team. They may even have some great pointers or thoughts or advice for you to consider.

But don't talk about leaving the military with your chain of command until you've taken the time to do your homework and to understand at least the basics of what this transition entails and to determine your initial game plan.

This guide will allow you to do just that, so read on!

OK, now we want you to learn to "speak the language." You've got to absorb as much as possible about this new world of corporate America. The best way to gain a better understanding is to start reading, watching the news, surfing the internet or spending time at the library to better understand it. As you read and learn about the new environment, you will discover that some aspects of corporate America (such as vocabulary, cultures, incentives and more) seem rather foreign and new, while others (personnel development, team building, leadership, qualities of effective teams, etc) seem very familiar. To be the best prepared, you will want to focus on the foreign areas.

Just as in military operations, it is important to gain an understanding of the objective before maneuvering to reach it. Consider this as your reconnaissance.

In the end, you will want to be able to answer the following questions:

- What excites you about corporate America? What are some of the current concerns of leaders in corporate America? How are they planning to respond to these concerns?

- What areas do corporate America and the military have in common? What aspects of corporate America seem familiar? What is different?

- Which industries, departments or occupations are starting to sound exciting to you? At what level of the organizations do you see yourself functioning comfortably? Team member or team leader?

Continue to review your initial timeline and adjust high level dates as you move along.

You must do three things in order to gain a better external perspective:

1. Learn about corporate America. Study it. Gain a better understanding.

2. Start to picture and actively visualize yourself in corporate America. How would you handle some of the current challenges or opportunities?

3. Build a bridge. If you have not done so already, summarize this experience by clarifying in your mind what you liked about corporate America. This is the reason that you are excited about making the transition. (Here's a hint: It's not because you will be leaving behind all of the things that you find frustrating in the military. If you have any, they are still likely to be around in corporate America!)

Learn about Corporate America

What's the best way to learn about corporate America? Well, let's start with what you've done in the past. When you left the civilian world and entered the military, how did you prepare? Who did you talk to? What was your approach? Look for current resources in your life that can help.

Family members (distant or close) and friends can be great resources. Do you have an uncle who is getting ready to retire from corporate America, or maybe a cousin somewhere? Do you have a friend of a friend who has recently completed their transition or maybe started out of college in a role or industry that interests you? These types of contacts can really help. Gather their contact information from family and friends and start contacting them. Email can make this really easy. Try something like this (with your own personalize touch, of course):

Dear _____,

As I reach my __ year in the military, I am considering a career transition to corporate America. I am working to better understand corporate America to be able to better plan my transition and would like your help. Could you give me your input and advice?

Please tell me about your role/industry and why you like it. What has been the key to your success? Please describe a good day and a bad day in your work environment. What advice do you have for me as I start out down this new path?

Thanks so much for your time, and I hope to see you at the next reunion! Hugs and kisses to the kids! [Of course, you should plan to personalize the letter as appropriate]

Yours truly,

_____

Just send this out and see what you get. I think you'll be surprised to find that many of the ups and downs of corporate America are very similar to what you experienced in military life.

During my transition, I was lucky to have my spouse on my team. He had spent about 10 years in corporate America and he gave me great advice: "If you are leaving the military to avoid any frustrations from the past, don't do it. Many of them will still be there." It is a great point to keep in mind. Many challenges that may face you in the military — such as dealing with difficult people, nagging bosses, poor communication or poor management (yes, I know... not in your unit!) — will also show up in corporate America.

The same holds true if you are transitioning from the military through retirement.

As you start to reach out to your family and trusted friends, you'll be developing your Transition Team. **Your *Transition Team* is the group of trusted friends and family members who have detailed knowledge about you and/or positions/companies/industries that interest you in corporate America.** They will be very helpful as you continue along your timeline to help to keep your progress on track. Ask these people if they would not mind if you reached out to them from time to time to ask for their input or advice as your preparation continues.

You may find that you have some choices in whom you approach to invite on to your team. If so, look for the most straightforward people. Look for the ones who you can trust to give you honest and valuable feedback on your performance and on your questions. Don't look for overly negative or overly positive people, but rather reality-based people. You will really benefit from having team members who will tell you directly and accurately where you are doing well and where you need to focus your improvement efforts. You will also want team members who will give you their down-to-earth perspective on their experiences in corporate America, so that you can be better prepared.

As my story above shows, spouses, or significant others, can be great members of your transition team. (Of course, it can also be a difficult time for them as they work to create a vision of their lives through and after the transition. See Appendix D for suggestions and advice to spouses working with you during your transition to corporate America.)

Try to branch out of your normal military circles to find your transition team. Look for individuals who have experience with corporate America, ideally with interviewing. If you are in a remote location or in a foreign country, don't eliminate people who can help at home. Use technology to help. Phone interviews obviously don't have to be locally run. Onsite interviews can easily be simulated through a webcam and audio link. (Check out www.skype.com or similar internet search result for free videoconferencing options.)

Other Resources

As you are reading and learning, try to absorb a little bit from all four media venues: books, magazines, newspapers and the Internet.

Time management will be very important as you go along. Consider downloading audio books or periodicals for playback on an MP3 player or on your laptop. You can purchase books on CDs and listen to them in the car or other CD player. This can add great flexibility, can be a time saver and can allow you to experience the books in more creative ways, such as while you are driving or working out.

Be sure to take a few notes while reading. If you are able to walk away from a book with even three or four or five new concepts and ideas on how to put them to work in your life, you are far ahead of the average reader! So, read (or listen) with that end in mind. Enjoy the book, but don't study it like you would prepare for a weapons or standards inspection. Find your top three to five points, make a note of them and move on. Keep your notes handy and available to review in the future, possibly before your interviews. I suggest using a 5" by 9" index card and tucking it away in the book so it is handy to review and you know where to find it. You may want to type up these notes at some point in the future, but this is not a big deal.

Consider a speed reading course or try listening to the audio books while you are driving or working out. Remember, that the concepts only matter if you are able to retain a few of them and find a way to apply them in your daily life. If you read every word but can't remember anything the next day or don't use it to improve your life or performance, then it was a waste of time!

To reiterate: Enjoy the book, but don't study it like you would prepare for a weapons inspection. Find your top three to five points, make a note of them and move on.

You'll have a lot of books to choose from, but to be sure that you are reading topics that are relevant for present-day corporate America. To discover what they are, do some research. Here are great places that I've found to look for currently recommended business books or periodicals (in print or downloadable):

www.amazon.com

businessweek.com

www.nytimes.com

www.google.com

www.audible.com

You'll find a lot of great books there on a lot of relevant business topics.

Here's a suggestion. Consider reading a book or two early on about "Change Management" or "Dealing With Change." That will help you from "day one" as you begin your transition and take the necessary steps to transition your career and change your life. As a second topic, look for a book on building a modern, consultative approach to sales.

In reality, you are already in the process of pro-actively managing change in your life! Change leadership is all around you and a very valuable skill to refine. Change leadership skills and experience will also be highly valued in your new role in corporate America.

Remember: Albert Einstein defined "insanity" as "doing the same thing over and over again and expecting different results."

The Importance of Visualization

As you start to gather this type of information, your picture of corporate America will become clearer. With a more detailed view, it will be easier for you to start picturing yourself or to *visualize* yourself in the new environment.

Visualization is powerful way for you to prepare yourself for this transition. Spend some time doing it. Close your eyes and spend a few moments seeing yourself working and interacting in this new environment. As you continue your preparation, your vision will become clearer and you'll get more out of the exercise.

During the visualization, questions may arise, such as, "What type of challenges will I face every day?" or "Who will I interact with every day?" or "How will I know if I am performing well?" Write them down. You will be able to answer these questions as you continue along your transition timeline. If not, you may want to take these questions along with you on interview day.

As you continue to read and to visualize your transition, you will naturally find yourself identifying with the challenges faced by corporate America. This is great! Think about how you will handle similar situations after your transition.

Build a Bridge

As you go along and continue to prepare for your transition, many questions will come up that seem simple but which will grow in complexity as you attempt to answer them. When this happens, think in simple terms. A great way to do this is to think in terms of a four-to-six-year-old. If you ask a four-year-old what do they want to do or eat or play, they won't make it complicated. They will think and answer in simple and clear terms. This concept can really help you when you start to get bogged down with any type of decision or problem-solving.

Let's try it! From what you've read and researched, what excites you about corporate America? An adult type response starts to consider all sorts of things...schedules, companies, maybe even vacation policies. A four-year-old, on the other hand, would be likely to distill it down to simpler terms and respond more quickly based on what got him/her excited.

If you think on a simpler level, you might find yourself excited about things such as, "talking with customers," "problem-solving" or "taking on new challenges." Complicated thoughts or responses are not always the best answer. Simpler thoughts can be simpler to get across or to communicate. Remember this! It works in a lot of situations.

When you were reading or listening to audio books or articles, which pieces did you find yourself really tuning in to hear? Which sections made your mind active and your pulse quicken? This is called "passion," and passion is something that sets the star performers apart from the average performers. In the end, think about what gets you excited — passionate! — and then practice to communicate it in simple and clear terms!

Determine Your Initial Position Type/Industry Type Goal

Let's try this same thought process when determining your initial goal. What type of position or industry interests you? Think back to your time in the military. What roles, duties or experiences made you really passionate and excited — those projects that you found yourself thinking about on your own time, away from the office, projects that you couldn't wait to bring to completion? These are also the projects and experiences that you enjoy telling people about.

Now, remove the position specifics and describe the role in general terms. Was this a team role or individual role? Were there technical aspects? Did you problem-solve on your own or in teams? What was your manager supervisor like? How did you interact with them to be successful? Was your daily schedule always the same or constantly changing? What was your role on the team? What type of leadership roles were the best fit for you?

Complete this exercise for a couple of the roles or projects that you really enjoyed and draw out the parallels. What are the universal traits that continued from one role or project to the next? *The description that you have just created is the description of a work environment in which you excel.*

Try to overlay this type of work environment on your future goal in corporate America. This vision will become clearer as you progress with your preparation and research, but keep this in mind: *The work environment that was the most satisfying to you in the military will be the environment that you should try to find in corporate America to make a strong start.*

You will do well in this environment as a civilian, just as you did in the military. Practice describing this environment now, so that you can share it with the hiring manager on interview day.

At this point, you may only have a general idea of what type of role brings together these traits that you've recorded, but that's OK. You will continue to refine this desired role as you work through your transition. As you continue to explore and read available job descriptions in corporate America, you will be able to use these universal job traits to help you decide which roles would be great for you. Remember — these are the roles that make you passionate and draw out your energy and creativity.

Think about the feedback that you received from friends and family members who responded to your request for advice. What did you think of their description of a good day and a bad day? Would you feel the same way in a similar type role? If not, this is likely to not be the best fit.

At This Point, Directions are Better Than Goals

I'd like to make a point here. Setting an initial position/industry goal can be a particularly difficult goal when starting out. For some it will be as simple as putting on a different uniform to do the same work, but for others, this will take some time. That's OK. Start with a general direction and work to narrow it down as you go.

If, as you near your transition date, it still proves to be difficult to nail down a specific goal, it is fine to "interview around" a little bit and explore your options. Be aware, though, that this approach can lead to a higher rejection rating.

Hiring managers have a unique perspective. They get to see a lot of candidates and consider them for the same positions. They get pretty good at understanding which candidates will excel in the environment and which ones will struggle in a short amount of time.

Don't let rejection bring down your efforts! If it's not a good fit, there is no better time to find out about it than during an interview, and it certainly is understandable for the hiring manager (who is immersed in the organization's culture and roles) to be able to pick up on this sooner than you can. The earlier the better! Thank the interviewers and move on with confidence.

Just to get you thinking: Interview Foreshadowing

During your interview, the projects and experiences that you enjoy talking about are the ones that you'll want to be sure to share. As you talk about it, your excitement and success will be written all over your face and the interviewer will share in this passion, and be excited to hear about it. You'll bring them along for the ride!

Another side note about phone interviews: Smiles are audible over the phone. If you've never realized this, give it a try. Smile and use facial expressions while talking on the phone. You'll be more effective in sharing your passion and excitement!

One last note: Don't forget to tell your transition team members how much you appreciate them!

Chapter One: Interactive

Chapter One: Get Started! Fight procrastination, do it now!

1. Describe your reading and development plan to better understand corporate America.

I will read _____ book(s) every month off of the recommended reading list, including

_____

_____

_____

_____

_____

_____.

I will listen to _____ audio books every month. I will subscribe to and read this/these periodical(s) _____

_____

_____.

I will spend _____ hours weekly surfing the Internet exploring corporate America (reading websites and annual reports, reading about investors' analyses, looking at financial projections and returns, reading about current events in the world of business, etc.). I will send letters/emails to these contacts to ask for their help with my preparation:

_____

_____

_____

_____

Other things that I plan to do to prepare for my transition: _____

_____

_____

_____

2. What are three things that you learned about corporate America that were surprising to you? _____

_____

_____

3. What are three things about corporate America that *excite* you?

_____

_____

_____

4. What are two challenges currently faced by corporate America? How would you handle them as a leader in corporate America?

_____

_____

_____

5. Describe the qualities of the role (s) that you've had before that made you passionate and where you delivered outstanding results.

_____

_____

_____

_____

6. Describe your initial industry/role goal in corporate America.

_____

_____

_____

+ Be sure that you've filled out your initial transition timeline and updated it.

Leaving the Military™ Transition Strategy

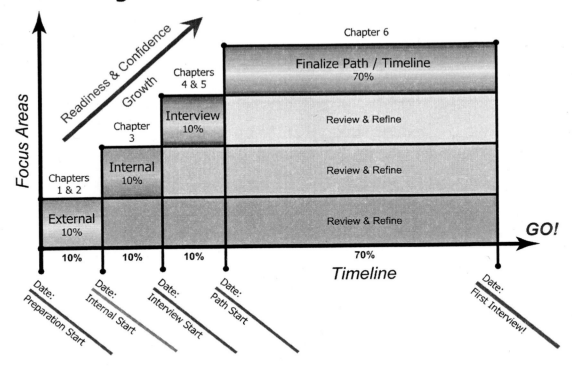

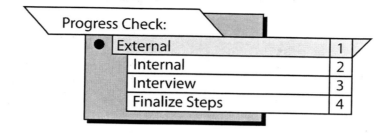

Chapter Two (External)

Learn about customers!

Let's start with a few questions for you to consider:

o Who are your customers?

o How do you identify and define your customers?

o What different types of customers exist and how do you respond to them uniquely?

o How do you know if your customers are happy?

o What other options are available to satisfy your customers' needs?

o How do you improve customer satisfaction?

o How do you make sure that you are continually meeting or exceeding your customers' needs?

o What did you think about these questions? Where they easy for you to answer? Did some questions seem as if they were "not applicable?"

If you answered, "yes" to this last question, please read this section carefully. All of the questions are completely applicable. You have customers in the military just as you will in corporate America.

By the way, this may seem like a pretty broad topic for the second chapter of a book on your transition, but this can be a difficult gap to bridge for some military candidates. It is mentioned here because it is very important for you to grasp. ***Corporate America lives, eats, and breaths for their customers, and it is a focus that you must learn and appreciate to be successful after your transition.*** The customer is king!

More background on the concept of customers is useful. If this concept is new to you, let's talk about how you see it every day in the military.

What are your customers?

For a word that is used so often in every day conversation, the word "customers" can easily be misunderstood. From the perspective of corporate America, a customer is anyone who derives value from your product or service, and there are two types of customers:

1. **External customers**: a person or group that is outside of your organization and provides payment to you or to your organization as a result of your products or services.

2. **Internal customers:** a person or group that is inside of your organization and relies on the output of your work to be successful. The quality of their work is directly related to the quality of your work, as they are on the receiving end of your efforts.

This breaks the word "customer" into two general meanings. The first is the more frequently used or common definition of someone who purchases or buys products or services from you or ***external*** customers. The second definition describes a person with whom you have to work with in order to provide products and services to your external customers. Let's call these ***internal*** customers.

Here's an example. If you work in Big James Bubble Gum Factory and it is your job to form the gum into small sections or pieces before they are wrapped, then your external customer is the person who goes to the store and purchases the gum and pays their hard earned salary for your product. Your internal customer, however, is any person that works internally to deliver the same product (bubble gum), but needs your work to be done before they can complete their task. In this example, the person who wraps the bubble gum would be your internal customer, as would the person who packages the candy as well as the person who takes the bubble gum order from the customer, and so on.

Now, with the same example, why is it so critical for you to think from the perspective of the customer? Well, what will happen if you don't? What happens if you start by ignoring or not being concerned with the needs of the external customer? For example, let's say you have one flavor of gum and you are satisfied that this is all that your customer needs. In today's global economy, customers have a lot of choices. Should the customer decide that they would like to try a new flavor that you don't offer, they will go to a new company and Big James will lose the revenue. If enough customers do this all at once, the company will not deliver the financial results expected and the stock price will fall. When the stock price falls, shareholders will want to know what the company leadership has planned to improve results. The response may involve a lot of things, including a renewed effort to deliver what the customer wants (new flavors?) or cutting costs (eliminating jobs or other expenses).

This is an overly simplified version of real life in corporate America, but it should be enough to get you thinking, if you haven't already, about why it is important to figure out what your customers (in this case, your external customers) want from your product or service and deliver it as soon as possible. In fact, you may be able to see in this example how many people proclaim that, "In corporate America, the only true job security comes from customer satisfaction."

So what about the importance of the internal customer? In the same scenario, let's say that Big James figures out that customers are tending toward a new preference with their oral indulgencies and decides to incorporate some new flavors. Marketing is sharing advertising with new flavors and external customers are excited. Now, if you don't pay attention to what the downstream internal customer, the wrapping station, needs from you, what will happen?

If the wrapping station will only support sectioned pieces that are a given dimension with a fixed tolerance, let's say +/- 10%, and you continuously deliver a variety of shapes and sizes that can be as much as 20% over the target value, what will happen? The wrapping station won't be able to wrap the bubble gum and will throw out the candy at a loss to the company or send it back to your station where you will have to stop the progress of your assembly line to re-work the item and bring it into tolerance. Also, while this effort is holding up the line, it is also reducing the output of the line and making the external customers wait. When customers wait long enough, they are likely to go elsewhere to have their need for quality gum with innovative flavors met by someone else (if the market supports it).

This simplified example shows the importance of both internal and external customers. After reviewing and thinking about these two definitions, it is difficult to picture anyone who is not a customer, or someone who is not really involved in an internal or external customer relationship. All throughout the effort to deliver quality products or services to the external customers, you will find a number of customer-supplier relationships, each of whom is dependent on the other to keep the external customer satisfied.

OK, let's apply this to your life in the military. Who are your external customers? For whom do you or your unit work? If you are in a transportation or aviation unit, your external customers are the maneuver or infantry units that value, or may even allocate costs associated with, your services to transport their troops into the landing zones or to the training locations. Think about who is, or should be, paying your bill. If you are a maintenance unit, your costs are likely to be allocated to the maneuvering or Infantry unit. If you are part of a maneuvering- or Infantry-type unit, you are working directly for the taxpayers and for the country.

We've determined that external customers are the groups that get value from or pay for your products or services. How about your internal customers? Who do you work with on a regular basis? Who is directly affected by the quality of your work? Have you ever thought of them as customers before? In this meaning of the word, you are working together with these individuals, and you must supply them information or quality work for each of you to provide reliable, quality results to your external customer.

In this way, they are your customers, and *you* are also *their* customer.

Yes, it sounds a little bit strange, but think about it. Internally, you are the recipient or "internal customer" of anyone else who is involved in your service chain to meet the customers' needs. The communication and teamwork required is a two-way street that requires everyone working together to stay on track and to meet and to satisfy (or, hopefully, exceed) the external customers' needs.

In the military, let's use the transportation or aviation unit example. Again, your *external* customer is the person or group receiving the end result of your work or your services, in this case, the maneuver unit or the Infantry. Your *internal* customers are all of the departments and related teams that you must work with to meet customer needs.

So, if you are transporting the Infantry unit in your UH-60 Blackhawk helicopter, some of your internal customers are:

— the aircraft refueling team: you'll need fuel to get there!

— the dispatch or flight scheduling team: you'll need a clearance to go!

— the supply personnel: you'll need your flight gear, uniforms and more to be successful!

— the maintenance personnel: you'll need to be sure that everything is in working order before take-off

...and so on!

Hopefully, this is painting a clearer picture in your head. In the end, you work together with your ***internal customers*** to satisfy the ***external customers'*** needs!

An interesting thing is likely to happen as you start to think of and acknowledge your internal and external customers for what they are. By formalizing your customer relationships in your mind and by acknowledging their dependence on you, and yours on them, you are likely to spend some time thinking about how you could provide better results.

Congratulations! This is exactly what corporate America is looking for in top candidates — someone who is aware of their customer relationships and is constantly thinking about how to better work with and serve the needs of customers.

If you have not yet left your role in the military, start to apply this frame of mind to your everyday life. Really think about your customers — both external and internal! Think about how you could help them to be more efficient. Think about how you could strengthen your relationship with them to allow you both to have better results.

As you continue your efforts from Chapter One and continue to read and learn about corporate America, you will read about the emphasis and value placed on relationships with customers. Continuously review and think about how you could work in your current role to enhance your relationships with your internal and external customers.

Here's an idea. Have you ever asked your customers for feedback on your performance? If not, why not? How do you know if you are doing a good job? Better yet, have you asked them to rate your performance on a numeric scale and then tracked these results over a period of time to determine trends? Give it a try! Yes, at first this may seem a bit strange in the military, but is it? Wouldn't a customer in the military care just as much — if not more — about the quality of service that you are providing to them as they do in corporate America? In a lot of cases, this customer relationship may be even more critical, as lives are not put on the line in corporate America as often as they are in the military.

On the other side of the spectrum, in some areas of the military, it may be possible to survive by simply satisfying your boss's needs. However, this will not work in corporate America today. Today's globally competitive environment requires that all individuals at all levels of the business must work together to satisfy the customers' needs. Again, it is the customer that really pays the bills and ensures job stability for everyone in the company. ***Only a concern for and desire to increase customer satisfaction can ensure job stability in corporate America!*** In most cases, customers have many options in the global,

Internet-based economy. It can be very easy for them to take their business elsewhere when their needs are not met. Of course, this is a little bit different in the military. Military units may have some latitude when it comes to choosing their maintenance or legal support units, but it is likely that they have limited choices.

In order to be successful with customers in corporate America, start thinking about your own customers now. Learn how to satisfy your customers in the less-competitive military environment to help you ensure your success in corporate America.

Take a moment to think about your summer jobs from your youth. Did you spend any time "flipping hamburgers"? How about working at a car wash? Many of the summer jobs that young people take during high school or college breaks can help to make a great connection between work and the importance of customer satisfaction for you and for potential employers. Keep these in mind as you prepare for interview day and don't be afraid to mention them as your earliest experiences in customer service.

Here's a couple more questions: What is the best way to communicate with your customers or to ask for their preferences or feedback in the military or in corporate America? How do you do this today? If you have any experience in sales or have read or talked with others in sales, you might have a "leg up" in answering these questions.

Sales

Before we look at ideas for this, let's back up and talk a bit about sales. What is your perception of sales? As you build your list of desired job descriptions or roles, did a role in sales appear? Why or why not? It is not always easy to visualize or understand the role of sales when transitioning from the military. While in the military, you may have limited experience in a sales role or even interacting with sales agents. You may be living off of pre-conceived notions of the sales role. ***If the word "sales" makes you think of pushy, slick car sales people in poorly matched suits, then you are off the mark. Sales people like these may be prevalent in the movies, but they are not the norm in corporate America today.***

As you start to read more about corporate America and the sales role, you are likely to hear terms such as "Integrity Selling" or "Consultative Sales." Both of these terms are getting at the same idea with the same emphasis. Successful sales people in today's corporate world work to understand their customers' needs or problems and then to find a way to satisfy them with integrity. Yes, this is a pretty simplistic description, and there is a lot more to a successful selling relationship, but I think it can be very helpful when transitioning from the military. It can also be very reassuring, for in an organization like the military, where integrity is at the heart of all interactions, sales is actually a career choice that won't violate your core beliefs and values.

Now that you've adjusted your picture of the corporate American selling environment, you may even want to consider adding this type of position to your desired roles listing. Look for any one of a number of bestselling books on the topic today. Enter "best selling consultative selling book" or "best selling integrity selling book" into your favorite internet search engine. Order the book that returns and read it for better understanding. Check out the suggested reading list in appendix A for a place to start.

Communicate!

A more accurate view of the effective selling environment may also help you to better answer the earlier question of how often and when to communicate with your customers. The bottom line is that your goal should be to talk with them *as often as possible* and to make this a pleasant and value-based experience for your customers. If your goal is to always find ways of increasing customer satisfaction, you should to talk with them in a way that is "easy" and "open." Be careful to not waste their time!

"Easy" should mean that you don't ask that your customer fill out a complicated form to give their feedback. It also means that you should go to their location to collect it. For example, you might attend their meetings, rather than requesting that they come to your location to attend yours. It is a subtle change that can mean a world of difference to your customers.

"Open" meaning that you encourage them to not hesitate to tell you about things that frustrate them. You may ask them questions such as, "How could

I/we do better?" or "What is your biggest frustration/problem area right now?", and then find a way to help out! You should establish very open communication, giving them easy access to you and your team to be able to talk and communicate.

Of course, you will also want to be sure that once you've asked your customers to take time out of their busy day to give you feedback on your product or service, that you actually use it. Don't just ask for the sake of asking. Make sure you know what to do to feed it back into the company to improve their level of support and ultimately, their level of satisfaction. Again, be careful not to waste your customers' time!

Customer satisfaction is the focus of corporate America. Start to apply this priority in your current role. Think about whom you work to satisfy every day and how you measure this satisfaction and improve it. You'll feel great about your improvements as you increase your customers' satisfaction and you'll create great examples for you to share and discuss during your interviews with hiring managers!

Chapter Two Exercises (Interactive)

Get Started! Fight procrastination! Do it now!

1. List your external customers: _____

_____

_____

_____

_____

2. List your internal customers: _____

_____

_____

_____

_____

3. List ways that you could work to strengthen your relationship and communication with your internal and external customers: _____

_____

_____

_____

4. What will you do to get input from your customers on your current level of performance and ideas/suggestions for improvement? (surveys, interviews, etc):

_____

_____

_____

_____

5. As a combination of the first two chapters, give one example of how corporate America is struggling to stay customer focused. How do they get customer input to improve their products or services? How do they use it: _____

_____

_____

_____

_____

6. What steps will you take to improve your level of understanding of the sales role and the sales process in corporate America? _____

_____

_____

_____

_____

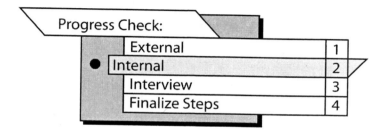

Progress Check:	
External	1
● Internal	2
Interview	3
Finalize Steps	4

Chapter Three (Internal)

Learn about you!

Let's look at this in two steps. First, you will collect and *summarize your military accomplishments*. Second, you will translate this list into *competencies* to learn to speak the language of corporate America.

Summarize Your Military Accomplishments

Start by collecting all of your military paperwork. Collect reviews from your roles and education. Collect awards, class completion certificates and certifications. You should be able to find most of this information through your branch of the military online personnel web site. Download and print out all of the documents and put them into a three ring binder. (You may have heard of this referred to as an "I love me" binder.)

Look For Quantifiable Accomplishments

Now, sit down with a highlighter or marking pen and mark up your documents. Look for quantifiable accomplishments and examples that you feel will translate well into corporate America. Just as you focus on quantifying your results with numbers when writing a military review, look for them now. Corporate America also values numbers and quantified results.

What is a quantified result and why is it important? This will not be new to many of you leaving the military service. The forms and rating systems may change often in the military, but the value of a specific statement of results does not. The goal is to get to the heart of the accomplishment with focused action words such as "improved," "conducted," "initiated," "collaborated," "accelerated," etc. The action word should start off the accomplishment and draw in the resume reader, and the quantifiable results, or the number, should help them to understand what was really accomplished and on what scale. Accomplishments can be quantified by things such as:

- Percent improvement
- Time saved
- Money saved
- Productivity increased (ability to do more with less)
- Cycle time reduced
- Quality increased

...and more!

This will become easier as you develop a better understanding of corporate America, but you will continue to revise this as you go along. For now, use what you've learned about corporate America and look for examples that you are excited to talk about. ***Look for experiences that you really enjoyed, that challenged you to step up to the next level or examples of how you improved your process or team results, maybe even accomplished***

something that had never been done before or improved your level of customer satisfaction. Just as these types of accomplishments are exciting in the military, the civilian world will be excited to hear about them as well.

Your Overall Experience in the Military

Take a few minutes after you've completed this exercise to think about your overall experience in the military. What was your favorite role, favorite mission and favorite unit? Again, describe it to yourself as an outsider looking in. Here are some more detailed questions to ask:

- Why did you like the role, mission and unit? What got you excited?
- Did you work in a team or as an individual contributor?
- What part of the accomplishment did you lead? Did you enjoy this part of the effort?
- Did you find a way to motivate the other team members to get them closer to the goal?
- What did you accomplish while at this unit? How does this compare to your other accomplishments while in the military?

Note that it is likely that the role that you are the most excited about is also the role where you had the greatest results. It just felt like the unit "clicked" together and was able to accomplish great results with less effort than others. That is why it is so important to determine what type of role and environment draws out your best performance. This type of role (with the same type of team or environment) is a great place for you to start with your civilian career. It will be a great place for you to show off your abilities and to be a star performer!

Continue down your list of highlighted accomplishments. What is your second and third best accomplishment? Develop a general description of the role, unit and accomplishments. Eight to ten accomplishments would be great to work with as you prepare for your transition, but complete six as a minimum.

Take this down through as many examples as you can. At first, write out these accomplishments in full detail on paper or on a computer. This will force you to recall and review all of the details behind the accomplishment. As time progresses, you will move from written examples to verbalizing them with a clear, concise and effective delivery.

Common Traits: Your "Competencies"

With this developed list of favorite positions in the military, look at them together. What common traits do you notice starting to develop as you look across all of them? What trends are you seeing?

Step out of your own shoes. Act as if you were reading this description of another person and try describing the traits from this perspective. These knowledge areas, skills and abilities are referred to as "competencies" in corporate America. Our goal is to map your experience and strengths into these categories to make it easier for you to communicate your abilities and goals to hiring managers in corporate America.

Many competency listings exist from different development programs. Start with the competency listing on the Department of Labor website at:

http://www.careeronestop.org/competencymodel/tool_step1.aspx

This website will give you a definition of each of the competencies for you to review. Feel free to spend the time looking at the overall competency model listed at this website as well, but don't get too bogged down based on your overall timeline. For now, you should select a handful of competencies that seem to tie in well with your accomplishments and work experience. Continue to review and refine this listing as you progress along your transition timeline.

What is the bottom line with all of this talk about competencies? Really, it is no more complicated than being able to categorize your strengths and your improvement areas. This effort will make it easier for you to have a conversation with corporate America in their terms about what they desire and what you can offer. Think about describing yourself to someone new. How would you do that today with respect to your professional accomplishments? Competencies allow you to draw parallels between your results over time to show strengths and weaknesses. They also allow corporate America a way to try to "match you up" into a role where you are likely to be happy and one in which you are likely to excel.

As a note, you are not going to find one standardized list of all competencies that are in use by all companies in corporate America. In the past, the Department of Labor has made an effort to standardize their own model and terms, but this does not mean that it is in use by all of corporate America.

Get organized! Make a Transition File

You may notice that you are starting to accumulate a "stack" of documents, magazines and binders related to your military transition. Let's get it organized. Find a small, expandable or portable file cabinet and label the individual sections. You may find that labels such as: "reading material," "ratings," "awards and certificates," "transition team input" and "companies and positions" will work well as a start. This will be your "Transition File."

In the past, I've noticed some consistency in strengths and weaknesses across successful military candidates. This listing of knowledge areas, skills and abilities is not taken from any standardized competency listing, but it will do just fine for you to use when describing your strengths and weaknesses to others and to get you started in categorizing them. Please don't take these as your own, but use them for ideas and to get you started. Again, you may find that some of these are strong traits for you, others are weaknesses.

- o leadership: direct and cross-functional (meaning across functions that are not necessarily assigned to your direct supervision)
- o critical and analytical thinking
- o problem solving skills
- o customer focus
- o initiative

- change leadership

- ability to work with a very diverse group of people effectively

- planning and organizing

- ability to communicate among individuals, peers and units

- counseling and developing others

- budgeting, being accountable

- ability to function and promote results in a highly diverse workforce

- "a make it happen" attitude — the ability to execute in difficult environments

- ability to perform under pressure (combat or other)

- technical skills

- risk analysis and mitigation

- business acumen (or comprehension level of business skills and environment)

Combine these ideas with the competencies listed on the Department of Labor website listed above or other competency listings. List the competencies that seem to be appearing repeatedly in your work experience and accomplishments. Develop a list of about ten competencies that are showing up as your strengths. Also think about a couple that are not showing up in a lot of places. These are your weaknesses. Document them as well and be prepared to discuss them.

Get Others' Opinion

Now that you have an initial listing of accomplishments and associated competencies that are displayed in them, let's get a second or third opinion. Call upon your Transition Team. Summarize the top military accomplishments and the competency strengths and weaknesses that you've identified from the accomplishments. Tell them about your favorite role and accomplishment and get their feedback. Send them some or all of your written out accomplishments and ask for their feedback on those as well. These are some additional questions for you to ask them (depending on their background):

- o Did I communicate my accomplishments clearly to you?

- o Are the competencies that I selected as strengths or weaknesses clearly displayed in this accomplishment?

- o Did I sound excited when I told you about these accomplishments. (This is not as natural as you might expect. Remember: if you are excited about the accomplishment, you want to be able to show it in your manner of communication).

- o Did I communicate this example in a way that will be clear and interesting to a corporate America Hiring Manager?

As you may notice, these questions are starting to lead you down the path of interview preparation. We will talk more about this later, but it is never too early to start preparing! Remember that you can have the most exciting and effective performance of any person in your military unit, but if you are not able to communicate it during your upcoming phone and in-person interviews, it won't matter. Start to practice and improve your communication skills now!

The Leaving the Military™ Competency Matrix

Let's look at a tool that will help us to visually summarize your work experience with your competency strengths. It is the Leaving the Military™ Competency Matrix. Look at this example:

Leaving the Military™ Instructions for The Interviewing Preparation Competency Matrix:

Step 1: Complete accomplishment/ competency match.

Weight:	**1a.** List accomplishments here:	**1b.** List competencies displayed here:					
		resulsts oriented	problem solving	relationship building	initiative	competency5	competency6
	Initiated imporved parts recycling program saving the unit $dollars annually.	☆					
II	Designed new maintenance plan that improved customer satisfaction level by XX%.		☆	☆			
I	Developed and led new training program resulting in XX% improvement.				☆		
I	Reengineered range planning process resulting in XX% trained, XX% above the standard.		☆				
	accomplishment5						
	accomplishment6						
	accomplishment7						
	accomplishment8						

1c. Place a " ☆ " at the intersection of an accomplishment/ competency match.

This tool is used initially to plot out the competency strengths displayed in your top six to ten accomplishments in a visual manner. Later, this tool (and its lower half of the diagram) will be used to match these accomplishments into positions that you are considering. This will be very useful as you prepare for individual interviews.

I found typical spreadsheet-type software programs to be useful in creating and updating this tool, but if it's not available to you, don't worry. Use pen and paper or open up a file folder and create your outline there, or write in this workbook. Try to avoid using a dry erase or chalk board unless you are sketching out a rough draft. Be it digital or pen and paper, you want a result that you can carry along with you in your Transition File.

List your accomplishments that you determined across the leftmost vertical column. List the ten competencies that you determined across the top row. Now, review each of the accomplishments and create a star or other mark at the intersection of each of the competencies that is displayed with the example.

For example, above you can see that under the accomplishment, "Developed new maintenance plan that improved customer support by __%," there is a star at the intersection with the competency "Relationship Building." This signifies that this competency was displayed by the actions taken to complete the accomplishment listed. Complete the top half of your chart in this manner.

The competencies that you identified as strengths should have more frequent "stars" or be the most common competencies among your accomplishments. If not, consider revising your top competency listing. This is a wonderfully visual way to show the mapping of competency strengths to accomplishments, and, therefore, your strengths.

You will notice that the second step of this model is to look at available positions and the competencies that are desired in each. So, in the end this tool will help you in matching your accomplishments to the role for which you are interviewing. We will look at more on that later.

You can start to see your profile as a military candidate developing, and you are starting to better understand yourself.

Interview Questions

These accomplishment examples and assessments of your competency strengths and weaknesses will become your basis for interviewing. We will talk in greater depth about interviewing, but to get you started, let's get you familiar with some interviewing questions.

Remember, interviewing is "where the rubber meets the road." You will either ultimately be able to successfully communicate your knowledge, skills and abilities, or not. We are working to prepare you for the former. Also, you will be more and more effective in each successive interview. You will learn that interviewing is an art to practice. It is also a skill that you'll have to make an effort to maintain throughout your professional career, as it is a skill that fades quickly without regular practice.

At this point, our transition preparation is focused on summarizing where you currently stand and then working to refine your interview delivery to corporate America. Once you've gone through this transition preparation, check out a couple of tools listed in the appendices to help you to better prepare for your transition to corporate America:

- ○ Appendix A: Recommended reading List — Books to read to prepare you for success in corporate America

- o Appendix C: "Leaning Forward in Your Foxhole" — Tips for proactively addressing the common weaknesses of the military-experience candidate entering corporate America

Remember that personal development and growth is a job that is never finished. Always work to improve yourself, your knowledge and awareness and your level of productivity.

Start practicing!

To get you started in thinking about interviewing, let's get you started practicing. We will talk about some common questions here, but you should also stop by your favorite online or brick-and-mortar bookstore to find some books with common interviewing questions. These books can be helpful with more in-depth information. Many of these books try to tell you about "the question behind the question," or why the interviewer is asking these questions. It is a good perspective, but don't take it too far. Most people who are interviewing you are working to determine if you will be a good fit in the company, not trying to catch you with a conniving question.

As you take your first step in starting to prepare for interviewing, let's talk more about this skill. As the *Leaving the Military*™ transition model suggests, you should be well on your way to practicing your interview skills when you are 20% of the way along your timeline. That means that if you have 10 months to prepare for your transition, you should start interview preparation two months into your preparation. This may seem pretty early, but it is a critical skill, and also a fleeting one. That means that even if you have some interview experience under your belt, if you haven't interviewed for some time, you can't expect to deliver "on the fly." Each and every time that you consider moving up or on to the next position, career or company, you will have to practice and rehearse these skills to be sure you are ready, so start today!

As a guideline, your interview preparation, just like any rehearsal, should get you into a situation that is as close to reality or "game day" as possible to ensure the best results. This is called "mock interviewing." Find a quiet, uninterrupted place, work with an acquaintance who is not overly familiar to you and pull a job description from the internet to use in rehearsal. The best way to do this is to start Internet surfing to find positions that are open and available. When you find something that interests you, print out the job description and take it with you to the mock interview. Ask for feedback after every session and participate in mock interview sessions as often as possible, working to fit in at least a half dozen sessions prior to your real interviews (more, if possible).

Practice Questions

Here are a few questions to get you started. Go over them in your mind and rehearse them. Practice responding to them in writing. Then, gather your Transition Team members and practice delivering your responses in person.

- o Tell me about a time you worked in a team. Please be specific. How did you lead the group to contribute toward the end results?

- o Think about a conflict you recently had to resolve. How did you influence your peers? How did you work through that conflict to a successful resolution?

- o Tell me about a difficult person (colleague, customer or team member) with whom you had to deal. What actions did you take to manage through?

- o What was your favorite job and why?

- o What are your long- and short-term goals? Additional responsibility? New challenges? Greater scope of duties?

- o What are your strengths and weaknesses? Give an example of your strengths. How do you plan to overcome your weaknesses?

- o Why are you leaving the military?

- o Tell me about yourself, i.e. Why did you make the life decisions that you made? School, degree, military, etc?

A great way to practice these questions is to make flash cards and verbalize them during a commute or while you are in the shower. Find ways to fit this practice into your daily life. It will pay off greatly in the end!

Also, schedule regular practice sessions with your Transition Team. Remember: all of the most impressive accomplishments in the world will not matter if you are not able to communicate them clearly and effectively!

Chapter Three (Interactive)

Get Started! Fight procrastination! Do it now!

1. List your top six to eight quantified accomplishments:

_____

_____

_____

_____

_____

_____

_____

2. List your top ten competency strengths and two competency weaknesses.

_____

_____

_____

_____

_____

_____

_____

3. Complete the top half of your Competency Matrix Diagram here:

Leaving the Military™

Interviewing Preparation Competency Matrix:

Name: _____

Date: _____

Step 1: Complete accomplishment/ competency match.

1a. List accomplishments here:

1.
2.
3.
4.
5.
6.
7.
8.

1b. List competencies displayed here:

a.
b.
c.
d.
e.
f.

1c. Place a " ⭐ " at the intersection of an accomplishment/ competency match.

Step 2: Complete accomplishment/ competency match for desired positions.

2a. List desired positions here:

1.
2.
3.
4.
5.
6.
7.
8.

2b. Copy competency list from above:

a.
b.
c.
d.
e.
f.

2c. Place a " ⭐ " at the intersection of a desired position/ competency needed match.

4. Describe your plan here for interview preparation. What other books will you read for sample interview questions? _____

_____

_____

_____

_____

5. Where will you practice verbalizing these questions (in the car, in the shower, while exercising, etc.) and with whom will you practice (Transition Team)?

_____

_____

_____

_____

_____

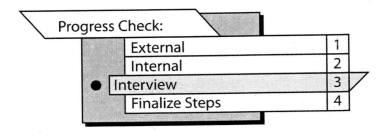

Chapter Four (Interview)

(Path) Build your action plan, development plan and timeline.

Just as you did with your initial timeline determined in Chapter One, start with the end in mind. Start by updating your transition timeline, indicating when and how you plan to conduct your first interview and when each transition section will be completed.

Plan conservatively. Again, let's look at the transition model:

Leaving the Military™ Transition Strategy

If it ends up that you have more time than expected, great. You definitely don't want to be caught short on time!

Write in the date that you would like to have your first interview (phone, career conference or in person) on the furthest point on the right side of your timeline. If you don't have any events or conferences yet selected, base it on your availability. Now, write in the date that you started your transition preparation the furthest point on the left side of your timeline. Calculate the number of weeks in between the two points and split them up according to the percentages listed in each of the colored blocks. For example, if you are starting your transition on Jan 1st and want your first interview on December 31st, there are 52 weeks to manage your transition. 10% of the 52 weeks in 5.2 or about 5 weeks for the "External" preparation. "Internal" and "Interview" are calculated the same at 5 weeks, leaving 32 weeks for "Finalizing Path/Timeline." Fill in these dates.

Now that your overall transition is in place, let's build it in some detail. Plan and schedule your time to visit your transition office on your base or post. This will allow you to schedule and plan, as needed, for PCS timelines, leave, movers scheduling, benefit planning and more. Your transition office can also be very helpful in finding open opportunities, interview preparation resources, counseling and much more, so plan them into the timeline!

As you plan for benefits, it may be difficult to plan out what will be your necessary income level for your first civilian position. In many cases your transition to the civilian world will be seen as a career transition and it is possible that you will take a pay decrease in order to get started in your new career path. For your first role, to the extent possible, put great emphasis on the experience and skills that you'll gain, as this will be an important role in defining the future path of your professional career.

The Personal "Profit and Loss" Statement

In order to calculate this or at least to understand what budgeting will be necessary for your new life, build a personal "profit and loss" (P and L) statement. In general, this will show your bottom line results as an individual and better prepare you to speak the financial language of corporate America. You will be better able to understand the financial backbone of corporate America, as most companies are built around combined business unit "P and L"s.

Use this format. (See below for some "notes on completing each line item.")

Personal Profit and Loss Statement

1. Income or net pay ($): $_____

2. Direct expenses or expenses directly related to your work or income on line 1.

(transportation, fuel, wardrobe, training, etc) ($): $_____

3. Gross Income ($): Subtract line 2 from 1 $_____

4. Gross Margin (%): Divide line 3 by line 1 times 100%   %_____

5. Indirect expenses or expenses not directly related to your work

(entertainment, travel, pets, housing, etc.) ($): $_____

6. Net Income ($): Subtract line 5 from 3 $_____

7. Net Margin (%): Divide line 6 by line 1 times 100%   %_____

Notes on completing each line item:

1. Income or net pay: this is what you bring in the door every month through your salary, retirement or other monetary income. In the world of corporate America, this will be your sales revenue from the amount of products or services sold.

2. Direct expenses: These are costs that are directly associated with your ability to bring in the revenue on line 1. Include transportation, wardrobe and cost of materials in this example, but be sure they are the costs that are directly related to your income. In corporate America, this will be costs to manufacture a product, or costs directly related with providing a service.

3. Follow instruction to calculate.

4. Follow instructions to calculate.

5. Indirect expenses: These are expenses that are related to the business, but not directly related to bringing in the income on line one. For your example, use training costs, housing or the cost of professional help such as an accountant or lawyer.

6. Follow instructions to calculate.

7. Follow instructions to calculate.

Again, this may give you a general idea of the appearance of your overall financial picture. Keep it in mind as you negotiate for salary and benefits or as you plan for your new income level. This will give you a basic picture of what adjustments will needed to be made at different income levels in your life. This example will also help you to think from the perspective of corporate America, which is always trying to maximize the bottom line (net income/margin) by increasing the top line (income or revenue) or by cutting costs (direct or indirect).

If this is your first time looking at a profit and loss statement or income statement, spend some time thinking about it. As you read through the financial statements of prospective companies online, review the income statement to understand it at a high level.

When you get into your first role, ask your leadership or financial team for an overview of the income statement and be prepared for the terms to shift slightly. Although this is a general guideline, not all companies follow the exact same outlines or use identical terms. In the long run, you will want to understand the company's individual "P and L" as it is usually used to score the financial results of a business unit and is the first focus area when talking about the financial strategy to turn around or to improve the profitability of the business unit. It is the bottom line of the local team and everyone must work together to improve the results.

Now, let's build some detail into your timeline.

You have created an overview and we will use it to drill down. Let's start at the rightmost point on your timeline again. With your completed research of corporate America, what companies have interested you the most? Did you discover any career fairs as you visited the ACAP office or did online research?

Many companies now have direct military-candidate hiring programs where your experience and leadership skills are recognized from the start. Watch for direct links from corporate hiring pages into military candidate-hiring programs. The point here is to identify a couple of hiring events or avenues that have peaked your interest so far.

Possible avenues include:

- ACAP or transition office recruiting events
- Veteran-based recruiting events run by a local employment or veteran service organization
- College-centered recruiting fairs, which can be found with an online search
- Industry-centered recruiting fairs, which can be found with an online search or by visiting industry focused trade groups

You can find listings of these events online by searching by region or by institution. Try to pencil in a couple of events that interest you to further focus your timeline.

You'll notice that I have not yet listed military-recruiting-company-run hiring events. We will talk more about these in future chapters. At this point, I recommend coming up with your own transition plan before reaching out to recruiting companies. Many military-candidate-recruiting models exist today and you will be more likely to find the right program for yourself if you've done some pre-work and laid out your initial plan.

More Specific Goals: Which type of company do you want to work for?

You should now be starting to think about more specific goals, and where you would like to end up at the end of this timeline. Think about this: Not all companies recognize military candidates in the same way. This can be a good thing or a bad thing, depending on your perspective and preference.

The companies that are familiar with military candidates and their strengths will show up easily. They are the companies that have the specific "hire from the military" link on their employment or careers website. They've hired military-experienced candidates in the past and have had great experiences with them. They will have the same expectations of you. They may even have a tailored post-hiring transition program that will help you in your adjustment from the military to corporate America. They have a better established understanding of what military experience means and how it helps you out as a candidate. They'd be less likely to harbor false negative impressions.

Once on board, you will find a good number of military alumni with whom to work and to identify. Is this a good thing? It depends on your perspective. On the surface, it sounds like a great thing. Any extra assistance in moving into your new role would be helpful.

Before you decide on a preference, let's talk about another type of company. This company has no special hiring links or hiring efforts for military candidates, but values your real world experience- military or other. They probably have hired fewer military-experienced candidates in the past and have fewer people employed who understand what it is like to make this transition. They may even be concerned (if they don't know any better) about your military past. They may wonder if you will come into the new role giving orders and shaking up the place.. .like they saw in some boot-camp-type movies or somewhere else. (You are less likely to run into these types of people in a company that hires and employs more military experienced candidates.)

For this company, you will generally find it easier to "stand out in the crowd." They may expect an average or normal performance from you, giving you a chance to shine. They are likely to be pleasantly surprised with your ability to "get things done." Unfortunately, with this company, you are more likely to run into military misconceptions as listed above.

In the end, it's all about preference and awareness. Do you perform better with high expectations and possibly more support or more mainstream expectations that allow you to personalize your adjustment and stand out from the start? Either scenario is manageable by learning to anticipate and respond to it uniquely.

Other Issues to Consider

As you are preparing for your transition, consider the impact on your family. In the military, your health care, vision and dental are all a part of your compensation. You may or may not contribute to a retirement savings fund. Everyone works toward a 20-year pension-type plan in the military.

In the civilian world, you will find a wide variety of benefits that may show up. Pay careful attention to **health care** as it is a growing issue in our country today and there are many concerns about cost containment. Many plans exist with a lot of variation and a lot of acronyms: HMOs, PPOs and more. Don't be too concerned about all of the options; just be sure that you and your family are covered.

Once you are covered, be sure to read the fine print in your specific plan. Some programs require that you always visit your in-network physician before going to a specialist. Others won't cover an emergency room visit to an out-of-network hospital.

Again, the bottom line is to be sure that you have medical insurance coverage and then to follow the guidelines in the plan. Unfortunately, this area of corporate America is not as simple as it is in the military.

As far as **retirement plans and pensions** are concerned, you won't find many pension plan options in corporate America these days. For the companies that offer them, many are looking at options for restructuring them or for cutting them back. 401k plans are pre-tax contribution plans that can help a lot when you are planning for retirement. They are also portable, meaning that you can take them with you if you should ever leave the company.

Watch for the employer's matching levels of these plans. Many companies will match the employee's contribution up to a certain amount every year. If you are offered this option, take advantage of it. It's a great benefit and and a great way to grow an accelerated retirement account. You may have to contribute on your own in order to experience it, so you will want to be sure that you set up your accounts to support the employer's matching contribution.

For more entrepreneurial or start-up type companies, you may be offered **stock options**. If you see these, you will have to read into the specifics as government regulation of these plans has become stricter over the past many years. In general, these plans involve being offered the chance to purchase company stock at a certain price at some time in the future. Usually, you will have to be at the company for a certain amount of time before your interest is "vested"' and you are allowed to "exercise" your options.

Education benefits can be included for employees and sometimes for family members. Benefits can be in the form of loans or gifts. Some benefits require the employee to pay them back if they do not remain at the company for a certain amount of time after completion; some do not. Some have annual caps on the benefit amounts. It is important to understand the specifics.

Relocation benefits may or may not be offered, with a lot of variation in their details. You may see anything from a lump sum amount (with taxes pre-paid or not) all the way to a full relocation with movers and home selling or purchasing assistance. These benefits may also be vested, requiring employer reimbursement if an employee leaves before a certain time. In many cases, you may be eligible for assistance from your branch of service for your last move after your final PCS. Keep this in mind. The military may cover the logistics of the move. In this case, it would be more beneficial for your new employer to offer you a lump sum to cover all of the other "incidentals" that go along with a move.

Many companies start all employees off at the same amount of **vacation time** per year. This can be a disappointing factor when you leave the military. My experience is that most companies start employees off at two weeks. Compared to the 30 days in the military, this sounds pretty bad. Keep in mind that all of your weekends and some of the federal holidays are not calculated in your vacation plans. Another nice perk... don't worry about what you do with your cell phone over the weekend. Many people in corporate America opt to check email or to connect with the office over the weekend, but it's not the norm. In general, it's a refreshing "work hard, play hard" type of environment where you are not on call over the weekends or evenings, unless by choice!

Just to get you thinking about the first days on the job....

Leadership

Like many other military candidates who join the ranks of corporate America, I at first was not quite sure how to approach my first few days, weeks or months on the job. I knew that I wanted to be a top contributor and to live up to or exceed all of the high expectations and promises that I had made on interview day, but I was not completely sure how to do this. I was not quite sure which skills would transfer and which skills would have to be adjusted or re-learned in order to continue to be a strong leader and team member.

To get to the point, I, along with many others, have found that little adjustment was necessary. In the military, it was possible for many to fall back on rank when motivating groups or individuals to complete projects or tasks, but I found out early (in the military, just as with corporate America) that this was not the best way to get the highest performance out of a group. The best way to get an individual or a group to perform is by helping them to be successful by accomplishing or surpassing their own goals, by facilitating their success. It was important that they were doing the task because they wanted to do it, not because they thought that I wanted them to do it.

This is an important point to be made about leadership in the military vs. corporate America. ***Leadership is leadership and the basics remain consistent.*** True leaders are successful in the military just as they are in corporate America — they succeed by helping their teams, peers and subordinates succeed. They inspire people to do things because they want to and because they care about the task or about the team, not because they've been given an order. In doing so, the leader and the team are able to look great together! Check out the book by John Maxwell listed in appendix for recommended reading on leadership.

Spend some time thinking about how you like to lead yourself or your team in the military. You can be sure, at some point, to be asked about your leadership style.

Stay focused!

As you continue your preparation for this transition, especially as you work your way toward interviewing, mock interviewing and peer coaching, you may notice peaks and plateaus in your performance. This always brings me back to sports performance. If you were on any college, high school or extra-curricular sports team, did you ever notice how, no matter how hard you worked, you saw more improvement on some days than others? Sometimes, on days when you worked the hardest, you may not have felt or seen any improvement.

Over the years, I've learned that it is at this exact moment — when you feel that you are continuously working toward improvement but are feeling none or even feeling a loss of performance — that you must dig in and stay focused. This seems to be the time when many people are at the highest risk of falling back and quitting. Don't do it! Recognize minor setbacks and a perceived loss of performance for what they are.. a stepping stone or 'breakthrough" point to your highest achievements. I like to visualize this performance using the chart on the next page.

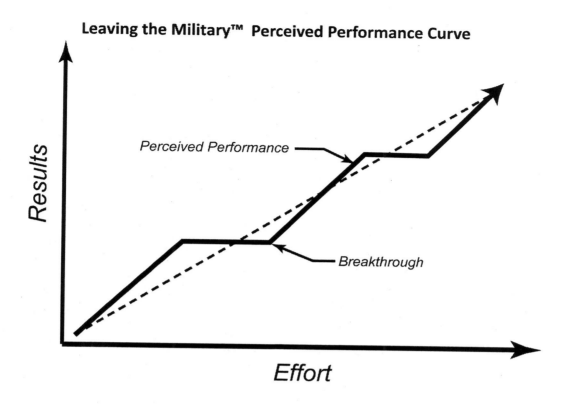

Leaving the Military™ Perceived Performance Curve

This chart simply reminds us to expect a certain amount of perceived acceleration and deceleration along our performance path. Some days require more effort to maintain the same level of growth. This can be a great time to elicit some input or encouragement from others to keep you on track.

Consider this chart as you work your way along your transition timeline. Remember that linear input does not guarantee linear growth or results. Expect ups and downs, but keep your eye on the final goal, have faith, and keep putting in the effort knowing that the results will follow!

Chapter Four (Interactive)

Get Started! Fight procrastination! Do it now!

1. List recruiting events and recruiting efforts (career fairs, networking events, resume submissions, etc) that you'd like to pursue along with associated timelines:

_____

_____

_____

_____

_____

2. Describe your specific transition plan and timeline from your branch of the service. Collaborate with your transition office to create and refine this. Include dates such as transition leave, travel dates, last date of service, family travel dates, etc. _____

_____

_____

_____

_____

_____

_____

_____

_____

3. Complete your personal Profit and Loss ("P and L") statement here:

Personal Profit and Loss Statement

1. Income or net pay ($): $_____

2. Direct expenses or expenses directly related to your work or income on line 1.

(transportation, fuel, wardrobe, training, etc) ($): $_____

3. Gross Income ($): Subtract line 2 from 1 $_____

4. Gross Margin (%): Divide line 3 by line 1 times 100% %_____

5. Indirect expenses or expenses not directly related to your work

(entertainment, travel, pets, housing, etc.) ($): $_____

6. Net Income ($): Subtract line 5 from 3 $_____

7. Net Margin (%): Divide line 6 by line 1 times 100% %_____

4. Describe your preferred work environment. Are you looking for a company that has an established program for on-boarding military candidates or a company that is new to military candidate hiring? _____

_____

_____

_____

_____

_____

5. Describe the benefits that are important to you and your family after your successful transition (health care, education, vacation, retirement savings, etc)

_____

_____

_____

_____

_____

6. Describe the benefit plan options that confuse you and your plan to get more information (401K plans, vacation, stock options, etc). Who will you ask? Where will you find the information?

_____

_____

_____

_____

_____

_____

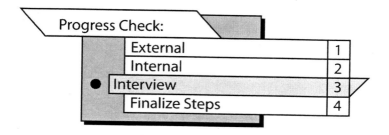

Chapter Five (Path)

Prepare your resume, interview skills and wardrobe.

Here it is! This is the "staging area" for your transition planning. You have now entered the sprint portion of your race, as you head towards the finish line.

But, first, let's review what you have already accomplished:

First, you spent time learning leadership skills and stockpiling incredible results in the military. You worked hard with a 24/7 mission and timeline and you made a difference.

Second, you considered transitioning and spent the first few chapters of this book exploring corporate America and learning more about yourself. You narrowed your focus and refined your timeline. Consider this for what it is... a very critical part of your transition.

Next: the three tools that will make or break the success of your transition!

Now, you will finalize the three tools that will make or break the success of your transition. Even if you've done the other two phases perfectly, it will be all for naught if you don't pay attention here. ***This third phase includes preparing the written, verbal and physical translation of your accomplishments and ability to perform in corporate America.***

- o Your resume is **the "written" picture** of you as a candidate. It is what will allow you to get time with a hiring manager on the phone or in person. It will also be the outline used by most of the people during your interview as they ask you about your results and accomplishments.

- o Your interview skills are **the "verbal" picture** of you as a candidate. These skills will allow you to properly communicate your impressive results and properly respond to all of the hiring managers' concerns and questions.

- o Your wardrobe is **the "physical" picture** of you as a candidate. This physical component will allow you to create the right first impressions and can be the "icing on the cake" that will get you the emphatic "yes" from the interview team.

One of the main goals of this section will be to prepare for your phone and/or onsite interviews. Practice and repetition is so critical here. It is so important that you practice communicating your results with energy, excitement and passion!

My Story

Now that I think that I've got your attention, I have a story that I've been waiting to tell you about my own transition as a great example of what *not* to do.

As I look back, my first few mock interviews felt like "night and day" when compared to my last mock interview sessions. I found that even though I had interview experience for different roles in the military, it was a whole new world for me when it came to preparing to enter corporate America. I had joined some transitioning colleagues at the military base library to practice mock interviewing. We had all prepared a few interview questions and notes and had brought along a video camera to capture our early results.

My turn was up somewhere in the middle of our group, and as I took my seat in front of our mock interviewer, I remember feeling very nervous, with sweaty palms and the like. As he asked a few questions, I answered. My answers felt choppy and not so rehearsed, but I thought I was getting my point across. I remember walking my way through the accomplishment details that I had read and talked through informally with my transition team. Everything seemed fine, that is, until I looked across the room at my interview partner.

He was sitting in the far back corner and had promised me to take some notes to share with me after the interview along with the other mock interview team members. Anyway, I looked over and saw his head starting to fall back and his eyes rolling back in his head. He was falling asleep! I couldn't believe it! I wasn't sure if I should make a loud noise or have a good laugh. In the end, the camera was rolling, so I continued and really thought about my message and how to communicate it succinctly and with energy.

What was the lesson I learned? That, just as your military training taught you (that if you wait until you are thirsty to take a drink, you are already dehydrated), if you at any point start to feel at all bored or lacking in energy as you tell of your accomplishments, you can be sure that you've already lost your audience.

That mental picture of my partner falling asleep has never left my mind. In any story that I am telling, I often put it to the "*Person in the back of the room*" test to see if I am including enough energy in my presentation and keeping it down to the key points without rambling. The funny thing was that as I looked back on the experience, I realized I was actually boring *myself.* I started to notice thoughts in the back of my mind such as, "What's the point?", "Where are you going with this?", and more.

(An author's note: My interview partner had actually returned from an overseas trip that morning, so possibly, the story was not as bad as it seems? Or was it?)

When you have time during an interview to start considering these types of questions, beware. You might be on your way to a "sleeping observer" response. Watch out for those! Again, if you are not excited while telling about your experience, your interviewer is not likely to be at all excited.

Use this equation

A (energy you include)**/2** = **B** (energy received by the interviewer).

Where:

A = the level of energy passion and excitement that you **add into** your delivery when talking about an experience, and

B = the level of energy passion and excitement that is **received** or **perceived** by the hiring manager or hiring team when listening to your response.

That means, **you've got to put in twice the energy, excitement and passion that you think you do in order to deliver your desired level to the interviewer!**

When interviewing, remember these three things:

1. Think about what you want to say and say it clearly and to the point! When asked a question, visualize the point that you want to make and then find the shortest path to get there. Start with the end in mind. Think about what you want to communicate and be sure that you do it clearly. Don't make it too short, but definitely err on the side of "Get to the Point!"

2. Talk in real-world examples. Don't talk about what you "normally" do or how you "like to handle" a situation. **Talk about what you actually did in a real world example.** Most of corporate America is set on competency-based interviewing and they will be looking for this. (More on Competency-based interviewing in a little while.)

3. Think about what was exciting with your story or experience or example and communicate your passion, excitement and energy about it!

Remember the equation: **A/2 = B**

At the same time, don't forget the basics as you interview. The bottom line is that you must answer the interviewer's question and that you should match it with one of your proudest accomplishments.

Visualize the Onsite Interview

As you continue to practice with mock interviewing, you will be better able to visualize your success with the onsite interview. Of course, no two interviews will be the same. Some interviews will have multiple people, while others will be with only one person. In some interview scenarios, you will stay in one room and the interviewers will come to you. Some hiring teams will provide you with an interview schedule ahead of time while others will not. Some interviews will want you to complete an application and some paperwork to bring with you on interview day, while others will not. The point is to practice as much as you can and then be flexible because each and every experience will be unique and exciting in its own way!

Beat your own drum!

Don't save your accomplishments to use later during the interview day. If you have an example that you are excited to share, do it! Remember your top accomplishments and be sure to spend some part of your interview discussing each one. Don't "save your best until last" because you might not make it through the entire day. Yes, candidates have been asked to leave half way through the interview, when the "fit" is not there from the start. Also, it is acceptable to use the same example with multiple interviewers; just be sure to mix them up as much as possible.

Also, don't let the interview day get away from you — it will go much more quickly than you expect. With your nerves on high and your "readiness level" maxed out, the day will scream by to completion. Make a point to talk about the accomplishments that excite you and that best display the competencies needed to be successful in the new role. We will complete the bottom half of the Leaving the Military™ Competency Matrix to help with this later in this chapter.

Closing an Interview

Now let's talk about closing an interview. If you've had a Sales Position in the past, this won't be a new idea for you. However, most people have not had a sales position in the past, so for a military candidate transitioning to corporate America, this can seem awkward at first.

In its simplest form, "closing" means summarizing your confidence that you are a good fit for the role while voicing your sincere interest in being considered for the role. This may seem like one of those "common sense" items to you. Why would you be in an interview if you weren't interested? Why would you have shown up in the first place? Trust me, it is not a given and hiring managers will wonder unless you clearly describe your level of interest to them.

Also, everyone loves a compliment, so take advantage of this opportunity to give them one. Tell the hiring manager or team leader about what you liked about the role, the team goals or the company. No, don't compliment them personally. In other words, don't tell them how much you like them, their clothing, hairstyle or anything else. (This may sound humorous, but it does happen!)

You will understand this as you gain experience on the other side of the interview table. Hiring managers may have a lot going through their heads. Your interview may not be the biggest event of their day. They have a lot of other things to think about. They are trying to deliver business results that contribute to the bottom line, delivering greater profit, greater quality or greater customer satisfaction. Similar to the military of the late 80's and early 90's, corporate America works in a Lean Global Economy that is continuously asked to "do more with less." In this challenging and competitive world of profit, they also have the problem of filling an opening on their team with a person suited to the job because if they don't it will impede their progress.

Don't get me wrong, the hiring manager really does care about you and wants to hear about your accomplishments, but he/she is also trying to remember what meeting follows the interview, which customer is trying to reach him/her while they are interviewing, and will they be able to make their goals for the week/quarter/year.

This gives you a clearer picture of why the close is so important.

Here are some examples of good ways to "close" an interview," but be sure to develop your own based on the situation:

"I've really enjoyed hearing about _____ project (or _____ goal or _____ challenges) and I really hope that I get the opportunity to show the team what I've got!"

"This is really a unique work environment in which I think I would thrive. I hope to get the chance!"

"You've really impressed me with the company's plan to _____. I hope to be a part of it in the future!"

I've heard the interviewing environment described as being similar to dating. This is a great analogy. Both you and the company are looking at each other for a good fit. You don't want to go out on the first date and have your date wonder if you enjoyed yourself and would like to continue. Especially in the business world, when you are interviewing, remove the doubt up front and tell them of your interest! Keep in mind, just as with dating, a vague or insincere complement can be worse than none at all. Think clearly about what you are excited about or impressed with and then let them know it with passion!

As you prepare for and conduct your mock interviews, use the forms on the following pages to score your results and to track recommended improvements. The first form is for your interview partner to complete after you complete a mock interview session. The second form is for you to complete based on your own performance following the same session.

Mock Interview Interviewer Score Card

(Interviewer, please complete.)

Date: _____   Time: _____

Interview Mode: _____ Phone _____ Live

_____ One on One _____ Team Interview

Interviewee or candidate: _____

Interviewer: _____

On a scale of 1 to 10, with 10 being high, rate the candidate in these areas:

____ (1 thru 10) Did the candidate clearly **communicate his/her accomplishments**? What was the most powerful example mentioned? What could have been improved? What competencies or strengths were conveyed?

_____

_____

_____

_____

____ (1 thru 10) Did the candidate **show passion and excitement**? What was good? What could have been done better?

_____

_____

_____

_____

___ (1 thru 10) Did the candidate clearly **answer the question that you asked**? What was good? What could have been done better?

_____

_____

_____

_____

___ (1 thru 10) Did the candidate **"close" properly** and **voice his/her interest in the position and the company**?

_____

_____

_____

_____

___ (1 thru 10) What was the candidate's overall results?

_____ Hire   _____ No Hire

Describe the major factors that influenced while making this decision:

_____

_____

_____

_____

_____

_____

Mock Interview *Self* Score Card

(Interviewee, please complete.)

Date: _____   Time: _____

Interview Mode: _____ Phone _____ Live

_____ One on One _____ Team Interview

Interviewee or candidate: _____

Interviewer: _____

On a scale of 1 to 10, with 10 being high, rate your performance in these areas:

___ (1 thru 10) Did you clearly **communicate your results**? What was the

most powerful example that you mentioned? What could have been improved?

What competencies or strengths did you convey?

_____

_____

_____

_____

___ (1 thru 10) Did you **show passion and excitement**? What was good?

What could have been done better?

_____

_____

_____

_____

____ (1 thru 10) Did you clearly **answer the question that you were asked**? What was good? What could have been done better?

_____

_____

_____

_____

____ (1 thru 10) Did you **"close" properly** and **voice your interest in the position and the company**?

_____

_____

_____

_____

____ (1 thru 10) Rate your performance overall. Which questions or areas seemed comfortable and which areas were uncomfortable (and need more work)?

_____

_____

_____

_____

_____

_____

_____

Preparing Your Curriculum Vitae (CV) or Resume

Now that you've gone over all of your ratings and highlighted your favorite and most quantifiable results, preparing your "curriculum vitae" ("CV") or resume will be pretty straightforward.

Remember that the military writing style that you learned in the military will serve you well in corporate America. Do you remember "BLUF" ("bottom line up front")? This will be a great carryover into corporate America to make sure that your most important points are prioritized and clearly stated. In effect, it means to get to the point concisely and clearly. As a note, Fortune 1,000 companies pay consultants and trainers thousands of dollars to pass this skill on to their employees.

Many resume formats and outlines exist. If you have time and are able, I recommend attending a resume writing class at a local college or transition office. Don't make it more complicated than it needs to be, just get started. In the end, if your resume is neat, free of errors, logically organized and if it clearly and succinctly communicates your results, you are successful. If you are not able to attend a class, here are some general resume building guidelines and formats to get you started.

General Resume Format

Your Name

Address (This should be the address at which you can be contacted, as well as the address from which you plan to accept employment. By assigning this address correctly, future employers will be able to factor in relocation costs early on, if offered.)

Phone Number (A cell phone number would be great. Make it easy for hiring managers to reach you, but be ready for their call!)

E-mail Address (Make sure you've got one and that it is professional. I recommend this format: firstname.lastname@freeonlineemail.com. Or, even better, remove all punctuation between names.)

Desired Position (This can be included if you are certain about the type of role that you desire, or if you feel that your resume does not send a clear message as to what career path makes sense. It is OK to leave it off of the document, but be sure that in your cover letter or somewhere in your communication you clearly spell out the type of position you desire. Personalize it to the company or the role that you are targeting, if possible.)

Work History

Dates Employed (List starting month/year of employment through ending month/year.)

Job Title

For each job you have had, give a "Job Description." (Talk about your responsibilities. Remember what you learned when you wrote military evaluations for yourself or for your team. Use verbs or action words, such as, "Responsible for..." or "Dedicated to...," but try not to repeat the same action words over and over. Consult your computer or an online thesaurus for help. Keep these descriptions brief and to the point (BLUF), but be sure to include the number of people that you supervised and the currency amount of the budget for which you were responsible. These numbers translate very well — almost directly — into corporate America. These numbers help the hiring manager cut through all of the acronyms and military jargon to be able to picture at what level you led in the organization.)

Accomplishments (Use a bullet format on the line directly below your job description section. Keep the bullets short, action- and results-oriented. This, too, should tie very well into what the military taught you as far as how to write military evaluation reports.)

(Continue this pattern of Job Description followed by action and results focused accomplishment bullets until you've covered all of your work experience.)

Other Activities (List here your leadership positions, awards and recognition, community service, professional society memberships and volunteer work. Include these items from your time in high school, college and/or the military. Prioritize the list. Keep it down to a few lines.)

Here are some additional **resume specific notes**:

- Cover all of your time. Don't leave gaps in your positions. Training windows should be included with one of your adjacent job descriptions/employment periods. As you look to accomplish this across years of military service, look for commonsense ways to group your experience. Group by rank or location or by type of unit, chronologically in time, without dragging out your experience to become too "watered down" and too lengthy.

- Keep it to one page. This will force you to prioritize your accomplishments. Just as with military evaluations, too much information only clouds up your true accomplishments. Think about your top accomplishments and make sure they are clearly described and documented in your resume wording

- No typos or misspelling allowed! Oh, that's right, you are coming from the military. I don't need to say anymore!

- Avoid military acronyms. More and more employers in corporate America are learning to "speak military" as they've hired from the military over the years, so they could not help but pick up some of the terms. However, even if one of the "regular" military interviewers has this experience and can look the other way or feign understanding when you talk about how "your MOS allowed you to receive an excellent FITREP and to PCS before the end of your tour," these people are few and far between and you will definitely lose another member of your interviewing team later on down the transition timeline.

- Add some flavor! ***Be careful to not fill your resume up with all sorts of military acronyms and terms, but do add some items that show the uniqueness and "flavor" of your time in the military. You've had an opportunity to do some pretty cool stuff. Talk about it!*** (For example, I had a friend who swears that she was given her first role in Hollywood working on the movie *Titanic* because the interview team was so impressed with her pistol qualification score. At this point, I don't recall if it was marksman or expert or whatever, but for some teams, like hers, it really peaked their interest and got her in the door!)

- A note to our more "seasoned" military professionals: I've recommended the all-inclusive date or "chronological" resume format here. Many military professionals who have retired and transitioned after 20 or more years in the service recommend an alternate resume outline. They recommend that in order to better prioritize and to better present the content of a full career in the military that you use a more skill-oriented or "functional" resume outline. In this format, you are not so locked into allocating every month of your past experience, but you can highlight your unique skill set.

Here are a couple of sample formats to help to get you started:

[**Sample** *Chronological* **Resume Format**]

Name
Address1
Address 2
Phone: Cell
email@email.com

EDUCATION
Degree (Year)
Major
University
Univ. Location

Degree (Year)
Major
University
Univ. Location

EXPERIENCE:

Date – Date – Company, Location
<u>**Job Title:**</u> Job Description goes here.
• See bullets below for some good "action oriented" starter words.
• Be sure to include quantified results with the numbers that quantify them.
• Keep the bulleted items short and to the point, just like military evaluation bullets.
• Be ready to talk about all of the bullets on your resume during the interview!
• Keep your resume to one page.
• Remove all extra spaces.
• No spelling or grammatical errors, at all!

Date – Date – Company, Location
<u>**Job Title:**</u> Job Description goes here.
• Led _____.
• Reduced _____.
• Developed, tested and deployed _____.
• Completed _____

Date – Date – Company, Location
<u>**Job Title:**</u> Job Description goes here.
• Exceeded _____.
• Removed _____.
• Created _____.
• Expanded _____

Date – Date – Company, Location
<u>**Job Title:**</u> Job Description goes here.
• Re-Engineered _____.
• Collaborated _____.
• Researched and enacted _____.
• Implemented _____

ACTIVITIES

<u>**High School:**</u> Sports, professional organizations, leadership roles, awards, and community events.
<u>**College:**</u> Sports, professional organizations, leadership roles, awards, and community events.

[Sample *Functional* Resume Format]

Name
Address1, Address2
Phone: cell
email: email@email.com

OBJECTIVE
To transition to a position where I can best use my: leadership, results focus, customer service and _____ skill set to benefit the company, shareholders and community.

Summary of Competencies Skills & Qualifications

- List here the competencies, skills and qualifications that you'd like to market to potential employers.
- These can be in paragraph format or in a bulleted list.
- They should tie in very well with the accomplishments listed below.
- Accomplishments below should list mostly recent (5 years or less) accomplishments with a couple from earlier.
- See bullets below for some good "action oriented" starter words.
- Keep the bulleted items short and to the point, just like military evaluation bullets.
- Be sure to include quantified results.
- Remove all extra spaces.
- No spelling or grammatical errors, at all!

Summary of Professional Accomplishments

Job Title: Job description goes here.
- Led _____.
- Reduced _____.
- Developed, tested and deployed _____.
- Completed _____

Job Title: Job Description goes here.
- Exceeded _____.
- Removed _____.
- Created _____.

Education and Certifications
- Degree, University, Location.
- Degree, University, Location.
- Certification or rating, Location.
- Certification or rating, Location.

Preparing for the Interview

Think of your first phone interview or onsite interview as "Game Day." If you've participated in sports in the past, you know that you want to have everything lined up before game day. This will involve as much practice and rehearsal as possible. Just as with sports preparation for Game Day, you want to practice in an environment as close to reality as possible and practice over and over until you get it right.

This is a great time to reach out to your interview preparation team. Get them involved in your practice. Nothing comes close to the level of preparation that you will achieve by mock interviewing. Plan for and participate in as many of these sessions as possible. You can look to your military base/post transition office for facilities to use. Many times they will have interview rooms which may or may not have video cameras to help you to tape and review your performance. This can come in very handy.

At first, you may have noticed that interviewing feels a bit strange. With so much talking about yourself and your accomplishments, it can feel like bragging. Talk yourself through this and get over it quickly. It is, in a sense, bragging, but everyone does it and you'll have to do it too in order to be successful.

Consider investing in a sample interview question book. Many have titles such as, *101 Common Interview Questions* or *Knock 'em Dead*. These books can be handy in preparing you for an interview. They will tell you about the typical interview questions and about some typical interview strategies that hiring managers use, or how to tell what is the "real" question behind the question that you are being asked. These books can give you a great insight into what the interviewer is thinking, in general, as they ask the questions. Keep in mind that some interviewers are more interview-technique savvy than others. Some really just want to know why you chose your major and nothing more complicated than that!

Another factor that you can plan for as you visualize the onsite interview, is that some interviewers will be more refined or experienced than others. Just as you are developing your interview skills, a new interviewer must develop his/her skill set. If some of your interviewers seem nervous, don't be surprised and do your best to set them at ease.

Mentally Preparing for the Interview

Let's plan in detail for Mock Interviews. What should they look like? What should you plan? The simple answer is to make it as realistic as possible. Since there is a very good chance that you've never been on a corporate interview (hence, your purchase of this book!), I'll describe it here. Let's talk about an onsite interview, since it is much more involved than a phone interview and requires a broader preparation and skill set.

A typical onsite interview is likely to last for an entire day. It is likely that you will receive the schedule of interviewers ahead of time, so you will have an idea of whom you are going to talk with. You will know how long each interview session will last and how long is planned for lunch or breaks.

You are likely to have instructions to go to a lobby and let the security or administrative person know that you have arrived. There is likely to be a place to leave your jacket or umbrella or travel items if you need to carry them with you. You will be given a security badge and wait for your contact to meet you. Be sure to plan your timeline to allow for your early arrival, at least 15 minutes early. This will give you time to use the restroom, freshen up and to be calm and prepared for the interview.

Your contact could be any of a variety of people: the hiring manager, the administrative person or a potential colleague. They will meet you, ask how your travels went and if you need anything (water, restroom or other) and then escort you to your first appointment. This first appointment may be with an interviewer or with a group of candidates. Many organizations will schedule interviews for the same (or different) positions with multiple candidates on the same day to minimize interviewer coordination and logistics efforts.

In your first meeting you are likely to be given an overview of your interview day. You will receive a schedule, if you haven't already. This will be your chance to ask questions about how the day is planned. You will want to be sure you understand the basics, such as where to be when and how you will get there.

At this point, you should also receive an overview of the company. If you don't get one, this would be a great time to ask for one. You should have a general idea of the company from the research that you've done ahead of time, but ask for more specifics if they are not provided. At the start, you will want to have at least an initial idea of how this part of the company fits into the big picture: corporate structure, customers, colleagues, etc.

After the overview, the same person or possibly the first person on your schedule (if these two are not the same) will kick off your interview. They will review your resume, compliment you on your accomplishments and start with their questions. Each interviewer or interview segment is likely to last about 45 minutes. Expect to be asked for your questions at the end of each segment and always have some ready. Questions show natural curiosity and interest in the role, two very attractive qualities at this point in the transition process!

The interviewer will give you time for questions and then head off to continue their day. You may stay in the same room all day or you may be escorted around to the various locations of the interview team.

As you go through your schedule for the day, you will likely talk with people who will give you a 360-degree view of the role and a broad view of the company. You will talk with your potential peers, your future manager (and with future subordinates, if you are hiring for a direct leadership role). During this exchange, each of the people, from their own perspective, will be seeking to determine if you will fit in the organization and be able to perform in the role, or not. Just as they seek to understand this, you should be conducting your own investigation to determine if you feel that you will be a fit and will be able to perform and excel in this role. Ask questions!

Remember, also, that everyone will have a vote in the end. Expect to be evaluated by everyone... that includes the receptionist, the operator, or even the cleaning or repair personnel! Everyone should be considered part of the team! Also, remember to take advantage of every opportunity to meet everyone and talk with as many people as possible at the new company and to learn from them.

As a military-experienced candidate with a great track record, you will be in great demand. Make sure you select a role that is a good fit for you and that excites you. It must be a win-win match from both the employee's and the employer's perspectives. You are both investing a great deal of time, money and effort down this future path.

At some point in your interview schedule, you will have lunch scheduled. This can be planned in a lot of different ways. You may spend this time with your potential future boss, or with a group of potential peers. You may go offsite to a restaurant. The company will pick up the tab and is likely to take the check. Be aware of your lunch choice, avoiding anything too expensive, too spicy or too difficult to eat. Be sure to show your gratitude and thank them for the lunch! During lunch, if the company is large and it's not already planned, you may want to ask if a tour could be accommodated. It can be very helpful to see the work areas and onsite amenities and can be a great way to help keep your energy levels up for the afternoon.

As you go through the day, resist the temptation to have a running scorecard in your head. Don't try to gauge your performance and try not to worry about it! The only thought that should be going through your mind is how to better prove your fit for and your excitement about the potential role. In the end, trying to score your results is likely to throw off your performance and may even backfire.

Most of the interviewers that you will experience will be very upfront. It is part of their job and whether they enjoy it or not, they usually have some compassion for the person on the other end of the table. After all, they were there themselves at one point, too. However, there are some people, whether planned intentionally to test your inner strength or out of their own free will, who will naturally or in a planned way come across as tough guys. It won't matter what you say to this interviewer; they are not impressed or overly interested. Don't let this affect or throw off your performance. Just be aware that they are out there and stay on track!

More interviews will be scheduled after lunch until the completion of your interview schedule. You will have to be careful after lunch, and as you reach the end of the day, to not allow your energy levels to subside. You are likely to end your day with the same person who gave you the orientation in the morning. It is unlikely that they will be able to tell you how the day went or give you any feedback on your performance at the end of the day, but ask for it. At a minimum, you must be sure that you don't leave without asking about the follow-up process. Ask these questions! What can you expect? Who will you hear from and when? If everything goes well, what is the next step? An offer? Another interviewer? Or other? Be sure that you know who to contact and how to reach them in case you have any questions.

Plan Your Mock Interview

Now that you have a better idea of how the day is likely to go, plan that into your mock interview schedule and use it for effective visualization of a successful interview day.

Your mock interview preparation should include phone interviews as well as interview scenarios with one or many interviewers. You are likely to have to perform in all of these environments before you are through, so get ready.

Spend some time before your mock interview reviewing and refining your transition goals. Review and update the initial roles and companies that you identified in your plan. Work to make your plan specific at this point. Look for example job descriptions online, possibly at www.monster.com. With your targets as specific as possible, take these company and position descriptions to your mock interview sessions and use them.

Select the accomplishments from your work experience that will prove that you have the ability to be successful. Remember the competency matching exercise that we did earlier? In order to prove that you can be successful in the new environment, select the accomplishments that best display the competencies needed in the new role. Many companies will actually list the competencies needed to be successful in the role. This can be very useful to your interview preparation.

In order to prove that you can be successful in the new environment, select the accomplishments that best display the competencies needed in the new role.

The Leaving the Military™ Competency Matrix:

Let's look at the Leaving the Military™ Competency Matrix again:

Leaving the Military™ Interviewing Preparation Competency Matrix:	Name: _____ Date: _____

Step 1: Complete accomplishment/ competency match.

1b. List competencies displayed here:

1a. List accomplishments here:	a.	b.	c.	d.	e.	f.
1.						
2.						
3.						
4						
5						
6						
7						
8						

1c. Place a " ☆" at the intersection of an accomplishment/ competency match.

Step 2: Complete accomplishment/ competency match for desired positions.

2b. Copy competency list from above:

2a. List desired positions here:	a.	b.	c.	d.	e.	f.
1.						
2.						
3.						
4.						
5.						
6.						
7.						
8.						

2c. Place a " ☆" at the intersection of a desired position/ competency needed match.

So far, you've completed the top half of this model. You've entered your proudest accomplishments across the leftmost column and listed the competencies displayed across the top right row. You created a star or other symbol at the intersection of the competency that is displayed by each of the accomplishments.

Now, we will move on to the bottom half of the model and enter the position(s) that you are considering. Skip a few lines underneath the last accomplishment that you have entered in the leftmost column. Now start entering each of the positions that you are considering in its own box in the far left column. Look at each position and compare it to the competencies listed across the topmost row, extending to the right. If the position requires the competency, add the symbol at the intersection of the position and the competency. Continue to work your way through all of the combinations of positions and competencies until you've considered them all.

Once Leaving the Military™ Competency Matrix is complete, it is very useful in interview preparation. Start at the bottom where you listed your considered positions. Move right across the line that extends out of the position box. Every time you find a symbol, move up to all symbols that are placed on the vertical lines. At each of the intersections, follow the line back left to the accomplishment that displays the competency.

If you create one tick mark on the accomplishment box and score this separately for each of the positions that you are considering, this tool will calculate a weighted priority listing for your accomplishments and tell you which accomplishments will be the most effective in describing your fit for the desired role. Talk about them first and talk about them the most often during your interview!

As a note, the ranking evaluation will be unique for each of the positions on the bottom half of the competency matrix. You may want to color code (or number) each separate ranking to distinguish the results, or complete a separate form for each position considered.

Let's review the instructions: (See next page.)

Leaving the Military™ Instructions for The Interviewing Preparation Competency Matrix:

Step 1: Complete accomplishment/ competency match.

1b. List competencies displayed here:

1a. List accomplishments here:

	competency1	competency2	competency3	competency4	competency5	competency6
accomplishment1						
accomplishment2						
accomplishment3						
accomplishment4						
accomplishment5						
accomplishment6						
accomplishment7						
accomplishment8						

1c. Place a " ☆ " at the intersection of an accomplishment/ competency match.

Step 2: Complete accomplishment/ competency match for desired positions.

2b. Copy competency list from above:

2a. List desired positions here:

	competency1	competency2	competency3	competency4	competency5	competency6
desired position1						
desired position2						
desired position3						
desired position4						
desired position5						
desired position6						
desired position7						
desired position8						

2c. Place a " ☆ " at the intersection of a desired position/ competency needed match.

Step 3: Analyze results, determine prioritized examples for interview responses.

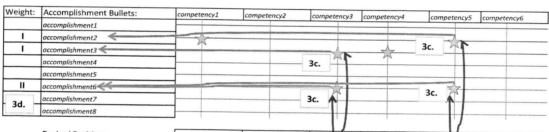

Weight:	Accomplishment Bullets:	competency1	competency2	competency3	competency4	competency5	competency6
	accomplishment1						
I	accomplishment2						
I	accomplishment3						
	accomplishment4						
	accomplishment5						
II	accomplishment6						
3d.	accomplishment7						
	accomplishment8						

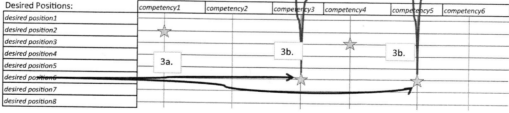

Desired Positions:	competency1	competency2	competency3	competency4	competency5	competency6
desired position1						
desired position2						
desired position3						
desired position4						
desired position5						
desired position6						
desired position7						
desired position8						

3a. Follow desired position from left to right to all intersection points (stars).
3b. Turn 90 ° and follow competency line up to all intersections on top half (stars).
3c. Turn 90° and follow line over to accomplishment bullet, make a tick mark.
3d. Tally scoring under each accomplishment. Higher scored accomplishments have the greatest weighted match.

* Plan & practice interview responses to match weighted scores.
* If possible, edit resume to reflect weighted scores.

Here's an example:

Leaving the Military™ Interviewing Preparation Competency Matrix Example:

Weight:	Accomplishment Bullets:	competency1	competency2	problem solving	competency4	inclusive leader	competency6
	accomplishment1						
I	accomplishment2			3.			
I	accomplishment3						
	accomplishment4			3.			
	accomplishment5						
II	accomplishment6					3.	
	accomplishment7						
4.	accomplishment8						

→ Accomplishment 6 shows your problem solving and inclusive leadership skils.

It is the most highly wieighted for the fireman position and should be a priority to discuss during the interview.

Accomplishments 2 & 3 should also be discussed.

	Desired Positions:	competency1	competency2	problem solving	competency4	inclusive leader	competency6
	desired position1						
	desired position2						
	desired position3			2.		2.	
	desired position4						
	desired position5	1.					
	Fireman						
	desired position7						
	desired position8						

→ A successful Fireman must display problem solving and inclusive leadership skills as determined by reading the job description or studying the position.

1. Follow desired position from left to right to all intersection points (stars).
2. Turn 90 ° and follow competency line up to all intersections on top half (stars).
3. Turn 90° and follow line over to accomplishment bullet, make a tick mark.
4. Tally scoring under each accomplishment. Higher scored accomplishments have the greatest weighted match.

In review, you started by completing the top half of the competency matrix. You matched your proud accomplishments on the left with the competencies that you listed across the top. You moved to the bottom half and filled in the names of the positions for which you are interested and planning to interview (mock or real). You made a note of the competencies that were needed in these positions by placing a star or symbol at the intersection of the role and the competency (again, in the lower half).

In order to analyze this data and to prepare for interviews, you started on the bottom left with the immediate position for which you are preparing and you followed it to the right until you ran into a star or symbol. Each time you found a symbol, you followed the competency line into the top half of the chart. In the top half, for every symbol on that specific competency line, you enter one tick mark near the accomplishment that is represented. Complete this for all of the competencies required in the bottom half and tally tick marks for the accomplishments that intersect in the top half. Talk about the accomplishments with the highest rankings during your interview sessions, again for that specific position.

Interviewing

Now that you know what you are going to talk about, let's talk more about interviewing.

I'll say it again (it's that important): smile during the phone interview! They can hear it! Smile during your onsite interview, as well. You may be nervous, but, remember, you want them to know that you are excited! Smiling is a simple act that can yield outstanding results!

For one on one, as well as team interviews, conduct mock interviews in both scenarios to prepare. Plan to meet as a group with your transition team. For the one-on-one interview, two people conduct the role playing and the remaining people can observe and score. For the team interviews, include everyone available up to about five people and allow everyone to ask questions and participate. The interviewers can complete their Mock Interview Score Cards while conducting the mock interview. The interviewers and hiring managers are likely to take notes as you go along, so it is great to get used to this.

There are different dynamics in the one-on-one and the team interview environments and you'll want to have experienced both ahead of time to build your confidence level. With group interviews, you can expect the interviewers to take turns asking questions. If you are dealing with a "competency-based" interview style company, each interviewer may be looking for different competency areas. One may be focusing on problem solving and the other may be asking questions, working to understand your level of technical competency. Don't worry too much about their strategy. Just go along with the interviewers and respond to the questions.

As you prepare, set yourself up as you will on interview day. For phone interviews, you'll want to practice and experience setting up your phone interview area. You should have a copy of your resume out to go over with the phone interviewer. You should also have a copy of the job description out in front of you with your notes, along with your completed, position-specific, Leaving the Military™ Competency Matrix. If you have a headset available use it to free up your hands. Your notes should be prepared to include specific work experience (examples) that you want to be sure to cover as well as questions that you want to ask about the company and the role. Write them out and have them in front of you

Plan for and conduct a dress rehearsal before the interview. This added level of detail will be very helpful and will assist in your visualization exercises. Wear what you plan to wear. Carry what you plan to carry.

I recommend that you carry a simple portfolio. Inside of it, include a blank note pad, a pen and a few extra copies of your resume. It's a great idea to have a copy of your professional references in there as well. You can also tuck away a copy of the job description, if you like, but don't plan to refer to it during the interview. In fact, it is really best if you keep the portfolio closed as you go through the interview, unless you need to write down some data such as contact information. I don't recommend opening it during the interview unless absolutely necessary, as this can break your concentration and can force you to lose eye contact with the interviewer. Both of these are detractors to overall performance. So, as you practice with the mock interview sessions, carry along your portfolio, but keep it closed, using it to hand out resumes or take minimal notes as needed.

Review: The Interview Questions

At this point, let's revisit the interview questions that you started with in Chapter Three. Take some time now to write down your responses to these questions. A few more questions are added to continue progress:

Tell me about a time that you worked in a team. Please be specific. How did you lead the group to contribute toward the end results?_____

_____

_____

_____

How do you work through conflict with peers, supervisors and subordinates? Give an example._____

_____

_____

_____

_____

Think about a conflict you recently had to resolve. How did you influence your

peers? How did you work through that conflict to a successful resolution?_____

_____

_____

_____

What was your favorite job and why?_____

_____

_____

_____

Why do you want this job? _____

_____

_____

_____

What are your long- and-short term goals? Additional responsibility? New

challenges? Greater scope of duties? _____

_____

_____

_____

What are your strengths and weaknesses? Give an example of your strengths.

How do you plan to develop your weaknesses? _____

_____

_____

_____

Why are you leaving the military? _____

_____

_____

_____

Tell me about yourself, i.e. Why did you make the life decisions that you made?

School, degree, military, etc? _____

_____

_____

_____

Who are/were your role models? _____

_____

_____

_____

What is your proudest accomplishment? _____

_____

_____

_____

Great Job! With each step, you are better prepared for game day!

Take some time to congratulate yourself. If you've never interviewed before, this is tough work. Interviewing skills are something that you will work to hone for the rest of your professional career. It is absolutely an evaporating skill set. Meaning that, if you don't practice, your ability will rapidly diminish.

Some Interview Recommendations

As you prepare for your interviews, I'd like to share a couple of areas that can really take down (and have taken down) potentially great military-experienced candidate interview performance and results.

#1: Talk in a language that the hiring manager can understand.

Again, you may find some team members who have military experience or for some reason are able to translate your acronyms and terms, but don't plan for it. General terms such as "platoon," "hanger" or "exercise" will work out OK, but stay away from terms such as "CO," "PT" or "ACAP." Just use the civilian equivalent. ***If the hiring manager or interview team can't understand your terms, acronyms or language choices, they will be concerned about your ability to communicate with the team once you are onsite.*** The hiring manager's goal from the start is to try to picture you successfully working and contributing to the team's goals. If the hiring manager can't picture you communicating clearly with the team, the odds are that he/she will not picture you as being successful.

A great way to think about this is to talk in terms such as you would when talking with your parents or siblings (as long as they have not served in the military). Think about the conversations that you have when you've gone home for the holidays and one of your aunts or nephews wants to know what you do for a living. In general, your translations should look something like this:

Military Term	Equivalent Civilian Term
CO or Commanding Officer	My boss
PT or physical training	Team exercise sessions
Division, Company, Squad	My team of about XXX people
OERs, FitReps, etc.	My performance reviews

I hope this list gives you an idea of how to talk through your acronyms and military terms in a way that corporate America will understand.

By the way, keep in mind that many civilian organizations have their own set of terms and acronyms that will show their face and probably confuse you a bit as you go through the interview. Be sure to ask about them and be confident in doing so. Having the confidence to stop the interviewer to clarify and ask about the terms used or the team is a great attribute!

#2 Talk with specific examples.

You will pick up pretty quickly the interview style of the group. Many organizations have formal training programs for people who will be interviewing external candidates. They are trained on the company's formalized approach to interviewing. This is likely to create patterns between your interviewers. We've mentioned competency-based interviewing. In preparation for these types of interviews, organizations look at successful examples of people performing in the role or a similar role and then list the knowledge, skills and abilities that make them successful. From this, they create a list of what competencies are necessary for hiring future successful candidates for the role and then look for those competencies on interview day.

Interviewers using competency models will be looking for specific examples of how you've displayed that competency in the past. So, for example, if you are telling an interviewer about how you like to lead people and you've gone through a very clear and to-the-point description of how you do this, don't think it strange when the interviewer cuts you off and says that it is great to hear how "you like to do something," but they need to hear about a specific example. Once you respond, you may even see them writing down the example for future reference. The bottom line is that you should expect to be asked for specific examples of how you demonstrated certain knowledge skills and abilities, such as problem solving skills, dealing with difficult people, or change leadership. Use your competency mapping tool to have the best examples ready for interview day.

#3 Be ready to think on your feet.

Many companies have tried unique approaches to show a candidate's ability to think on their feet. These questions show up as: "How many basketballs will fit in this room?" or "How would you weigh this airplane" and any type of question that talks to you about people on one side of the bridge trying to cross with or without any accompanying tools or items. My advice here is for you to have fun with these questions. Take it seriously, but don't break down in an overload of stress. That's really the only wrong answer with these questions.

This is a great time to remember that you've spent months or years negotiating complicated and hazardous obstacles in all sorts of terrain and foreign countries. You certainly can handle talking your way through this word problem! Again, the only way to really goof this question up is to stress out and close up. The best way to handle it is to get up on your feet, go to the dry erase board and start talking your way through it as you go. A bonus of this method is that you will probably get some inadvertent feedback from your interviewer or interviewers as you progress. It really says a lot when you have the confidence to get up in front of a group and talk your way through the problem. Watch for the tone of voice and body language coming from the interviewer or interviewers. This may give you much needed feedback as to the correct or incorrect direction of your approach.

#4 Be ready for team interviews.

Once you make it onsite, you may find that one or all of your interviews will be with more than one interviewer. We've talked about planning this into your interview scenarios. If you've been to promotion boards in the military or to flight school verbal testing, you will have no problem with these interview scenarios. If you find yourself getting nervous, remember that this team is just a group of everyday employees who put their socks on the same as you do every day. They probably went through this very same experience when they came into the company as well. Sure, they will push you a little bit to find your limits, but your rehearsals will have you prepared and ready to shine!

#5 Prepare everything that is needed prior to interview day.

Most military candidates have no problem with this, but, in the rush and excitement of interviewing, don't forget to follow all of your hiring manager's instructions! If they ask you to complete an application online, do it ahead of time with no errors. Take all of their requests seriously. They may seem not so important at the time of the request, but hiring processes can be very complicated, and if the hiring team decides to go forward with making you an offer, you don't want to be the cause of any delay. Prepare a list of actual professional references that you can take along on interview day or have ready to provide on request. Good examples of professional references are people whom you worked with in a professional capacity, such as military colleagues, peers, leaders, advisors, or members of the community with whom you worked or volunteered. Check out their contact information ahead of time to be sure that they are available and can be reached. You don't want to slow down the hiring process by listing out-of-date contact information. A great way to test this information is to contact them ahead of time (by phone or email), letting them know that you'd like to use them as a reference and make sure that you receive a response and that they are agreeable and available (in the country) to act as a reference in the near future.

The bottom line is that when you receive instructions from the interview team, follow them explicitly. Some may seem strange or not all that important, but you probably don't understand their hiring process, so just do it! Also, have all of these things (references, applications, resumes or other information) prepared and gathered ahead of time. Don't leave anything until the last minute or certainly not until the day of the interview. It is difficult to dig yourself out of showing up late or unprepared for an interview. Take advantage of a positive first impression.

#6 Don't start negotiating too early.

This may not be very intuitive at first, especially when transitioning from the military where all benefits are clearly spelled out and publicized to all. The point is that it is your job is to prove your "fit" to the hiring team right up until the last minute, until they make the decision to extend you an offer. You will know when that time arrives because they will give you an offer. Until you have something in your hand, your job is not finished. You need to clearly communicate all of your knowledge skills and abilities by describing examples that will convince the team that you will perform and will be successful.

Prior to receiving an offer, you are being evaluated and considered for the position. All opportunities to communicate with the group will feed data points into the decision. What does this mean? It means that you should not start negotiating — asking about the salary, vacation timelines, or other benefits — prior to receiving an offer. You should ask all sorts of questions, as many as you might have, about the position, the people and the team, how you will be evaluated or any other questions about the role. However, you should not dwell on or try to negotiate anything benefit-related at this point.

If you consider this from the hiring team's perspective, it is especially important while on an onsite interview (to the hiring team *and* to you) that you spend every moment learning about the company, the role and the team. If you spend this time asking about pay and benefits, you've created a missed opportunity to learn about the role and to share information to prove your fit. Without a successful interview and extended offer, you will feel pretty silly that you spent so much time focused on asking about the 401K plan and wonder if you could have told them more about what makes you a great candidate.

Prematurely focusing on the benefits also makes it looks as if this is your true concern. Successful organizations know that although benefits are important, they do not determine your ability to perform or to be happy in a role.

Your fit for the role and the company must be clearly displayed and determined before focusing on benefits or any type of negotiation.

Also, for you and for the company to determine if the role will be a fit from both ends, you must exchange a lot of information. Reserve the time for this. Once you have an offer in hand, you will have as much time as you need to negotiate salary and benefits, so wait until then. Many companies will provide benefit-related information to you during the interview process. Hold on to it to carefully review and consider prior to accepting or declining your employment offers.

Keep in mind these common military candidate mistakes. By planning ahead, rehearsing and avoiding them, you will be able to stand out in the crowd and make it successfully to an offer in hand!

Things to Do Before Interview Day

Now, let's move from focusing on what *not* to do, and talk about more things to *be sure to do* prior to interview day.

#1 Research the company prior to interview day.

At a minimum, you should have the basics down on the company and on the role before you voice your interest. You may not understand all of the product lines and all of the divisions of the company, but you should understand their general business model and their high level customer base and have an idea of where they are headed in the future. This information is necessary for you to properly gauge your initial interest and make sure it is a potential good fit for you.

So, what does this overall process look like?

1. You find a company and an open position (We'll talk more later about recruiting partnerships that you can create to help to discover this).

2. You research the company, to include:

   a. Revenue level (Are they on the Fortune 50, 100 or 1,000?)

   b. Customer base (Who are their customers? Where are they located? What is important to these customer groups?)

   c. Global footprint (Are they local or global? Where are most of their employees located? Where are they looking to expand?)

   d. Recent press (This can be as simple as running various Internet searches to find out what's going on with the company.)

The initial research can be done rather quickly and should be completed before any formal conversations with the company, such as a phone interview. ***If you make it to the point of going onsite for an interview, I recommend downloading their most recent annual report and paging through it to give you great perspective and insight into the company and its leadership.*** Be sure to read the message from the CEO at the front, and review the marketing material (usually upfront as well) that will give you an idea of the branding and image that they are trying to portray. Read over the financial data too to get a feel for the profitability and possible financial challenges of the company.

#2 Prepare your interview wardrobe.

In general, you should dress conservatively and in business formal attire, meaning a business suit and other appropriate attire. You should buy at least one reserved interview suit with 2-3 shirts that will accompany it. It is great if you are able to find a place to purchase these items together and try them on before taking them home. Many upscale vendors will offer free alterations with the purchase. Slight adjustments can make a big difference on interview day!

For women, this means a business suit with pants or skirt. A skirt (at or below the knee) will dress it up a bit further and is preferred. The suit should be of conservative darker colors, but, in general, avoid black. That can be a little bit too formal. A collared shirt worn underneath is a great look. If possible, try on the combinations before purchasing. Make sure the collar line of the shirt blends nicely with the jacket when they are folded out over the suit lapels or sits nicely when folded in. Keep jewelry and makeup to a minimum and look for a conservative, professional hair style.

For men, choose a conservative suit, shirt and tie. Again, avoid black, but look for a darker color. Polish your shoes. Be sure to have a conservative, professional hair style and be on your way!

For men and women, be sure to wear comfortable shoes that you will be able to wear for the day. Be prepared to walk. They may offer (or you may want to request) a tour of the company facilities. Take advantage of it! Walking around the location can give you great insight into what daily life is like for the workforce. It is likely to prove to be a valuable piece of information when you return home and are trying to decide on which company and position with which to move forward.

The bottom line here is that you want to be noticed as a professional package in your entirety. You don't want any one feature to dominate your look, such as hair, tie, jewelry or other.

It's also advisable to plan for the flexibility of taking off your suit jacket at different points in the interview. You can really go either way with this. I've noticed that men are more likely to take advantage of this than women, but, for most interviews, it is acceptable. Just watch for the cues that you get from your interview team. If they are all at business casual or less and you are out to lunch in a casual environment, go ahead. However, in general, I recommend that you wear your jacket for the duration of the interview unless it is a hot environment or you are uncomfortable.

If you've still got questions and need more detail, stop by the library or local book store and pick up a recent guide to dressing for an interview. This will give you the most up-to-date ideas on what to wear and what not to wear in more detail than you'll ever need. Try to find a recently published book with pictures, which can be very valuable here.

As you may be traveling out of town for these interviews, plan for it. Don't check-in your interview suits — carry them with you on the airplane, so that you don't have to deal with lost luggage. If your travel plans allow, don't wear your suit on the plane. Accidents can happen and you want a crisp, clean and neat appearance when you arrive. Also, bring a backup shirt and accessories (such as stockings or panty hose) to be ready for contingencies.

At this point in your transition plan, take a look at your initial timeline that you set in Chapter Three. Review and update it for accuracy. Adjust your preparation plan based on the timeline. If you thought you'd have four months until your first interview and now it looks like two, be realistic and adjust your timeline, but don't skimp on this chapter (Chapter Five). Resume, Interviewing Skills and an Interviewing wardrobe are all necessary before any interview. Get them done and then spend any additional time refining your interview skills. Interviewing is an art and you can always make further improvements.

Chapter Five (Interactive)

Get Started! Fight procrastination! Do it now!

1. What help do you need to complete your resume/CV? When will you have it complete? _____

_____

_____

_____

2. Who will you work with on your Transition Team to do mock interviewing?

_____

_____

_____

3. List your schedule and timeline for mock interviews. When and where will you meet? Include the type of interview being practiced (phone, single person or team interview): _____

_____

_____

_____

_____

_____

_____

4. Describe what you will wear to your interview. If you don't have all necessary items, when will you shop and where? _____

_____

_____

_____

_____

5. What interview book(s) will you buy/have you bought to help you to review interview questions and their meanings? _____

_____

_____

6. During your preparation so far, which questions or interview scenarios are the most challenging for you? What is your plan for additional practice and preparation? _____

_____

_____

_____

_____

_____

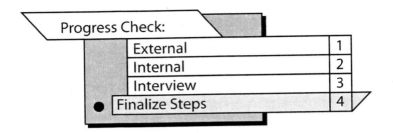

Chapter Six (Finalize your path)

Consider a partnership with a military recruitment firm.

As you work to network to increase your options, use all available opportunities. Look for local career fairs and for more traditional options: your alma mater, friends or acquaintances, and family members are a great start, but also look to the newer forms of technology-enabled networking, such as social networking and www.linkedin.com. A current search on your favorite search engine will give you some ideas of where to start.

So far, the transition path for most people has looked very similar. At this point, you will start to notice a lot of variation. That is because this is the *right* time on your transition path to consider working with a military recruiting firm. A lot of different options are available.

Why shouldn't you have considered this any earlier? The individualized preparation that you've done so far will help you to be sure that you choose the correct model for assistance out of all of the options. By waiting until this point in your transition timeline, you are more empowered to discuss alternatives, make the right selection, and to lead your transition effort in your desired direction.

Using a Recruitment Firm

The business of placing military candidates with corporate America is very lucrative. Recruiters can be paid anything from a fixed fee up to 20% or 30% of your first year's salary to place you in a position that is the right fit for you and for the company. Recruiting firms are expensive. None of their fees should ever be paid by you but should be covered by your future employer if a match is made. For you to be able to get the most out of this transition and have the highest success rate, it is better for you to consider your options and your desired career path well before engaging with a recruiter.

Please remember that the service cost of the recruiter should be paid by the hiring company and never by you. Some service providers exist that will offer to help to prepare you, to coach you and to get you to interviews, all at a cost to you. Although they are likely to provide a value, I don't recommend this approach. More than enough options exist for you to obtain the same result without any out of pocket costs.

Because of the cost of the recruiting firms or because of the confidence an employer may have in their internal recruiting efforts, many employers do not use recruiting firms — they prefer to find candidates on their own. During your early exploration of options available in corporate America, you are likely to have seen these companies. Some of them are very large corporations that see the value of military experience in their diverse recruiting goals and hire a lot of veterans every year. They may even have an entry program with some type of rotational or transitional program directed right at veterans.

Other corporations, big or small, that do not use recruiting firms just have not seen the value in the past. They may have a lot of military experience at their company and they may not. In this case, it is great to research this online before embarking upon the interview process with the company.

If you've targeted a particular company or hiring group, it can be difficult to find the right way to get your foot in the door to be considered. Networking and asking around is a very good option, but you will find companies that approach the questions of where to accept candidates in very different ways but for the same reason. The usual thought process used for decision-making is to consider the ROI or "Return on Investment." That means how much money do I have to put in for the same outcome or financial return? The problem is that different companies calculate cost very differently. They may believe that the cost of the recruiting placement fee looks small compared to the indirect costs associated with lost time for unsuccessful interviews, or vice versa. The point is that no two hiring groups will find candidates the same way.

Some hiring groups become so entrenched with a recruiting firm that they become very dependent on it. I've been in groups where candidates have placed their resumes in public online submission websites to never hear a response. Once they found the right recruiting firm, the candidate was considered and eventually made an offer for employment. The hiring group for one reason or another was not interested in candidates until they had been screened and recommended by their trusted recruiter.

Other hiring groups will explore all other options before signing up to pay the seemingly high recruiter placement rates. For these companies, online resume submission is likely to work well. As you can see, there is no one universal path to "getting in the door" at a desired company. The general rule is to be prepared, be patient and most of all be persistent! If one path does not work, but you feel strongly about the opportunity or the company, try another.

As we explore the different options, to determine which type of relationship is right for you, keep in mind your transition goals and how much preparation assistance or "hand holding" you would like throughout this process. This is the number one area of differentiation with recruiting groups. There are advantages and disadvantages for all of the different recruiting models, but a great way to keep them aligned in your mind is to remember how much preparation assistance each one provides throughout the process.

From the perspective of corporate America and the hiring manager, one type of recruiting firm can bring the same level of results as the other. It is likely that their "hit rate" or candidate placement success rate does not vary a great deal for the different established recruiting models. Of course, they would prefer to hire from a firm that provides the highest quality candidate at the lowest price. (As a note, they may actually make higher offers to candidates that come in with a lower recruiting fee attached to their employment agreement, with the same cost to them, within their hiring structure and guidelines. This is something to keep in mind as this candidate has a lower total cost of hiring.)

The bottom line with all of this is, of course, that the real determinate of your success in the interview and in the transition process is the amount of preparation that you complete. This is the easiest variable for you to control. Each model of recruiting partnership will give you a different mix of candidate/recruiter involvement, but the bottom line remains the same. **You will get out of this process the same level of results and commitment that you put into it.** Just think about how much "hand holding" you would like along the way.

Preparation Assistance

I will refer to the term "preparation assistance" with each of the models, so let's talk more about this. Preparation assistance is the amount of individualized help that you will get *before* the interview process. It includes things such as mock interviewing, work shop sessions, phone conferences and training sessions. Many of the recruiting models that you may encounter will not vary much once the initial match has been made to start the interview process. They will all be very professional in communicating with you and with the company to finalize the interview timeline and any travel plans necessary to get you onsite when you get to that point. So, remember: **the recruiting models vary mainly in the amount of assistance that you will receive prior to your first interviews,**

as everyone will professionally and meticulously work with both you and the company during the interview and travel window.

At a high level, many recruiter type arrangements exist and really depend on your goals during the transition. Again, you should never pay for the recruiting firm's services as this is something that will be covered by your future employer when a match is made.

Four Levels of Recruitment Firms

Let's break recruitment firms down into four groups that progress from a high level of control and preparation assistance down to a lower level of control with less preparation assistance.

Level One: Exclusive Agreement Recruiters

These types of recruiters will usually find you while you are still in the military. They may schedule on-base information sessions or use mass mailings to generic type military roles on the active duty installations. You will know that you've found this type of recruiter because, once they get through their sales pitch of "what's in it for *you*?", you will find out that there is some type of an agreement at the heart of the relationship. The agreement binds you in some way to consider their offered positions first or to use their services first before venturing out on your own. They are also likely to highlight their exclusive program that only accepts a certain (low) percentages of applicants who come their way.

This type of recruiting firm is likely to spend a good amount of time talking about the exclusivity of their group. Not everyone is accepted and they are proud of this fact. They may describe the placement advantage of their type of agreement. The assumption is that if only a certain number of "the best" candidates are accepted into the program, then they are better than the average candidate and will fare better during placement consideration or interviews. They may use this description to paint a picture of how you have an advantage over other military candidates making a transition that will allow you to start at a higher position.

On the positive side of this relationship, you will find this to be a recruiting organization that will be available to you as you prepare to transition. As early as two years prior to your leaving the service, they will make themselves available to you to answer questions, conduct workshops and get you ready to transition (Including help with mock interviews, location, timeline, wardrobe decisions and more!). These groups are looking for candidates who can spend some time preparing with them. The good news is that they will spend time with you in return, helping to coach you to a successful position in corporate America. Of all of the models, they will spend the most time and show the most commitment working with you to coach and improve your transition preparation level. They will take a certain amount of ownership in your preparation and work to help you plan for and complete your successful transition timeline.

They will check in with you from time to time and encourage you to complete certain items as you progress along the path to your transition date. You will likely sign up for some type of conference event with them near the end of your time in the military, carefully planning for available leave and PCS timelines. Many fellow candidates from their program, as well as subscribing companies, will attend, looking for you.

The hands-on type of preparation and coaching offered by this type of recruiting firm can really help to get you prepared during your transition, and it is really a good fit for someone who likes to have everything defined. As we looked at earlier, nothing will prepare you for the transition and for the interview as well as hands-on, in-person activities such as mock interviewing or interactive group workshops. (You will want to be certain to include these types of events in your preparation timeline, on your own, if you do not opt to go with this type of recruiter.) Be sure that your preparation includes receiving performance feedback to gauge your development and readiness level to interview. Reflect on yourself and your preferences to know how much hands-on interviewing and preparation will directly benefit you.

These firms are also likely to have standing relationships with companies for which they recruit in corporate America. This can be an advantage as they are able to give you a good idea of what to expect from the interview with the company, and maybe even with the interviewers themselves! You should expect a good amount of help from this type of company in understanding your targets in corporate America, as they have dealt with them before.

On the negative side, these types of organizations can be rather overbearing. With so much invested, they will push you along their transition path and along their process without a lot of back and forth consultation. They will want you to follow their process without much room for flexibility and they may resort to pressuring you from their end to keep you on their desired path and timeline.

If you've spent a good portion of your time up until now thoughtfully considering your options and preparing, and are confident in your decision, you are not likely to find this to be a problem. You may want to head exclusively in a direction (industry and position) that is fully represented by this recruiting firm. If so, then that is a great fit.

If, on the other hand, you stumble right into this group, and commit to them, their transition preparation can be a bit too aggressive and too controlling. Pay careful attention to the type of positions that they are filling, in which types of companies, as well as the types that they are *not* filling as there is not likely to be much flexibility in this area. If you are not yet certain as to the general direction of your transition, you will not feel at ease when transitioning with this group.

Carefully consider before using this type of relationship and go into it with your eyes open and communicating openly. What is painted to be an exclusive organization may end up to be more controlling than you would like.

Level Two: Moderate Support Recruiters

With this type of recruiting firm, you will notice the exclusivity agreement fade away, and you will see less ownership of your progress along your transition timeline. You will find more of a consultative relationship between you and your recruiting partner. The recruiter is likely to explore possible career options with you as well as possible career path directions, but only to a certain point, as it will be important to them to keep the process moving.

These recruiters are also likely to have a list of clients in corporate America with whom they normally work and should be able to give you an overview or "threat briefing" to help you to be better prepared for your interviews. They won't steer you down any particular path but will only have certain clients available. They will not push your progress as well as others firms will, but they are likely to have a number of resources available to you to help you through your transition. These will come in the form of anything from checklists to written material to limited in-person events. Take advantage of this assistance, but take the leadership role in this relationship. Ask for assistance where you feel you most need it.

These recruiters are likely to get involved in preparing for interview day, but not as extensively as the level one recruiters. They will help to interface with the hiring company to be sure your travel arrangements are complete and acceptable to both sides. They will also have some valuable insight into the hiring team and role.

Remember to leverage the recruiter's position when working with any of these models. This is one of the most important reasons to consider using a recruiter — they can make it a lot easier to communicate with potential employers. Whether it is from the start in understanding the details behind a job description, or at the end in trying to understand why an interview did not end up with an offer, a recruiter will be able to get more information from the hiring group, which he or she can share with you for preparation or learning, than you would be able to on your own. Recruiters use their consultative sales skills to understand the needs of their clients in corporate America. In doing this, they gather a lot of information that will be helpful for interview preparation and for a review of "lessons learned" after an unsuccessful interview.

The positive side of this type of recruiting agreement is that you are free to work with whomever you like, other recruiting firms included. You can look at and consider online available positions and know that you are not violating your agreement. You will also feel less pressure or control from this group. You will be strongly encouraged to advance along your own individual timeline. This type of military recruiting group may find you outside a local military base, or may be easily located with a simple Internet search.

The negative side is closely related: Without the individualized "hand holding" of the first model, you may find yourself procrastinating or letting your timeline slip as you get closer to the interview date.

Be honest with yourself as you consider these models. ***If you are a die-hard procrastinator, look at the more controlling models (or a good study-buddy) to keep you on track and be sure to follow your Leaving the Military™ transition timeline closely!***

Also, as strange as it may sound, you may not receive enough or much negative feedback from this interviewing model. At first, that might not seem like a bad thing until you consider that negative feedback is the most important way for you to make improvements in your performance during the interview process. It is very valuable to hear about what's *not* working in your interview preparation or interview style *before* the actual interview. If you aren't receiving any negative feedback, be sure to ask for it!

Again, the power of this recruiting model is that it leaves you with more control over the process than the level one model does. After working through the previous chapters of the Leaving the Military™ transition process, you are already well prepared (with room for improvement) and have a good idea of where you'd like to go in corporate America. This recruiting model can be a very good match as long as you take advantage of the assistance provided by it. Just remember: you will have to be more vocal in asking for their help and suggestions. After your mock interview sessions, ask for their input on areas for improvement.

Level Three: Limited Support Recruiters

This type of recruiting relationship does not offer a lot of development or one-on-one interaction. They may offer more of a list of available positions rather than any type of recruiter helping you to prepare. They will expect you to have the basics down and be ready to go.

This group is also likely to have a list of usual clients and it is not unreasonable to expect or request an overview or preparation briefing prior to interview day to assist you with your preparation. Ask them for advice or additional background to better prepare you for interview day with the company. If they have been around for a while, they should have no problem providing it. Overall, you won't see a lot of commitment to you (in terms of individualized time spent with you) from the recruiters themselves. They are likely to have goals of attaining a certain amount of "throughput," that is, of candidates resulting in placement.

If you work with this group, you will see a lot of variation in the amount of service provided to you as a military experienced candidate transitioning to corporate America. It is really best to just ask up-front questions to determine how much support they will provide, such as interview preparation or travel plan preparation, when considering the use of their services.

Level Four: Hybrid Support Recruiters with Non-exclusive Agreement

This is the best model for recruiter partnerships. It pulls together the best of the past three types to create an environment that provides the highest return to the military candidate transitioning to corporate America. The effort put into streamlining the communication between the military candidate, the hiring manager, the recruiter and with peers who have transitioned down a similar path before is what really makes this model stand apart.

This type of organization brings together the best of all three of the previous models, including:

- o the hands-on participation and guidance of the exclusive-agreement model

- o individualized feedback on transition preparation and readiness

- o the clear path outline and clear expectations, as with the exclusive and moderate models

- o the support and consultative environment of the moderate recruiting model

- o the fast-moving and flexible environment of the limited support model, to be used if needed during an accelerated transition timeline

The Hybrid Recruitment model also includes some additional advantages:

- o more easy access to and feedback from corporate America hiring managers and hiring groups

- lessons learned from "mismatches" are fed into the process in two places: in the determination of a hiring manager/group compatibility for the transitioning service member and into the description of hiring goals of the hiring team
- attention paid to the hiring group to determine their readiness level in accepting the military candidate to determine if transition assistance and preparation is needed on their end
- access to program alumni who can share advice and network

This can be a great program for a variety of participants, as it can be easily tailored. This model includes a generally recommended transition timeline with personalized milestones and interactive triggers to help to keep individuals on track. It also includes personalized interaction and interview preparation through peer or facilitated group coaching sessions.

As this is a hybrid approach, I encourage you to "interview around" a bit with varying recruiting firms to better understand their approach. If they don't do exactly what you like, ask if they will. Make the request. They may not have provided the same level of personalized attention that you are requesting because no one ever asked for it! In doing so, you will create the recruiting model that works the best for you, your transition strategy and your timeline.

Or you can go it alone.

It is also not uncommon and perfectly acceptable to "go it alone" or to transition without a recruiting firm's assistance. However, if you are leaving the service with no civilian work experience under your belt, this can seem rather intimidating and should be carefully considered. I strongly recommend that if you elect to not use a recruiter on your transition team you find other external resources (such as the military transition assistance office) to help you to successfully chart your course out into the open water of corporate America.

Do What's Best For You

If you are approaching your transition timeline and are still uncertain if a recruiting partnership is right for you, I recommend that you give it a try and look for the model that you believe to be the best fit. In the end, with all that you have on your plate as a candidate transitioning from the military, you are likely to find the expertise, advice and assistance to be worth the effort in setting you up for success in corporate America.

Once you've gone through the earlier steps of the Leaving the Military™ transition process, research specific recruiting options by going online and asking around for recommendations. Choose one of the models that works the best for you and give it a try.

If you choose any model other than the exclusive model, you can explore opportunities on your own at the same time that they are looking through their list of clients and positions, searching for a match. This can expose you to more than twice as many companies than if you were purely doing this on your own. Remember that with whichever model you select, you will get the most out of the transition process when you take ownership of the plan and draw in other professionals to assist you as you need it or to augment your development curve.

There is a tremendous value that the "right" recruiter can bring to you in your final steps of transitioning. These recruiters from all available models see many military-experienced candidates every day and can share very valuable feedback with you on an assortment of things. It is important that with whichever model you choose that you find a recruiter who will be open and honest with you throughout the process. You want to make sure that you are able to have two-sided conversations with the recruiter and ask any questions that come to mind.

Remember, as this is your first time going through this process, you are going to have questions and you'll want to be able to ask them openly in order to be successful with this transition. A recruiter who is too controlling, trying to push you in one direction, is not the best option. Neither is a recruiter who is so "hands-off" that they will sign you up for an interviewing opportunity before confirming that it is a good fit for you and for the company and that you are adequately prepared. The recruiter should feel a certain amount of personal responsibility to be sure that you have a basic understanding of the company and the role to be successful.

A great way to weed out the less effective or less experienced recruiters is to ask them about their placement rate. How many military experienced candidates did they send out for an interview and how many of them returned with an offer in hand, or eventually received an offer? This data will be a great way for you to rank the effectiveness of each recruiter.

How You Can Get The Most Out of the Recruiter-Military Candidate Relationship

Let's walk through this process a bit to map out how you can get the most out of the recruiter-military candidate relationship. Here is the process outlined with some key actions to take to get the most return from your recruiting relationship:

- **Choose a recruiter:** Select your recruiting firm. Get input from your Transition Team, if possible. You are likely to find the contact or "request information" form right on their website. Fill it out and complete it.

- **Initial contact:** Ask them for an overview of their recruiting model and how they will be compensated. Listen to how they respond to this question. Be sure it is an open and comfortable communication environment. If it is not, find another firm. Ask them about their history in military recruiting and transitioning. What data can they provide? #'s placed? Firms represented? Industries represented? What support and feedback will they offer as you prepare for phone and onsite interviews?

- **Voicing your interest**: Early in the conversation, they will ask you about your goals. Based on your transition efforts so far, you should be able to answer this question, but ask for their thoughts or advice and consider them. Remember, they do this every day and will be able to tell a lot about you and your likely match. Ask for their advice and incorporate it into your plan!

- o **Ongoing interaction:** Every interaction should be considered as an opportunity to present yourself, much like an interview. Ask them for their feedback on this as well. How are you doing and what could you do better? Phone conversations can be very valuable. It will be great to understand how you are coming across on the other end! Be sure to ask them to determine what they consider to be your strengths and your weaknesses as a candidate from the perspective of their corporate client base. Compare these with your own list. Ask them about "best practices" or military candidates that went before you that did outstanding? What made them great? What can you learn?

- o **Considering options**: At some point, you will have to make some decisions, whether it is the choice between who to select on an interview schedule or the choice of which offer to accept. Ask for their advice. Don't ever allow a recruiter to make your decision for you, but do take their input and consider it.

Follow-up Communication

Another point to consider when thinking about recruiters is that they are likely to play a very large role in the follow-up and negotiation point of the interview process. We will talk more about interviewing follow-up later, but, for now, know that the recruiter can really earn their keep during this timeframe.

Here are some examples of follow-up communication where a recruiter can be a big help:

- **Determining results of an interview**. Liability concerns may prevent a company from providing any detailed feedback on your interview performance or your fit for potential companies to you directly but the recruiter may have access to more candid feedback. Ask your recruiter for this feedback. Ask them to give you as many details as they can and to be as "up front" with you as possible.

- **Receiving and analyzing an offer.** They may have some insight into what offers have come from similar companies for similar roles and be able to help you to determine how attractive the offer really is.

- **Responding to multiple offers.** They may be able to help facilitate your decision as to the right position with the right fit. In the end, this must be your decision, but they've been through this before and can help you to ask yourself the right questions to find the right answers.

- **Negotiating with the company after receiving an offer.** They can be the right kind of middleman to help you to make your way through this part of the process and to be sure that everyone is smiling when it is all done.

- **Turning down an offer.** At this point, this may seem like a wonderful problem to have, but you want to be sure to handle it in the right way, in a professional manner with careful and timely communication.

Let's Review Your Transition Timeline

Now that you have a fair understanding of the services that you can expect from a recruiting partnership, let's review your transition timeline for accuracy. Review your detail with a high level of accuracy and make sure it's right. This timeline is likely to be one of the early points of discussion with your recruiter.

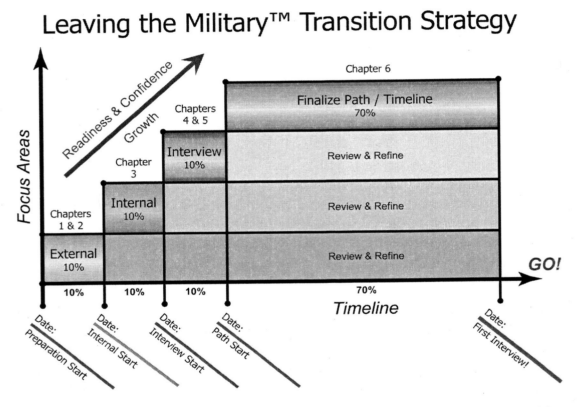

Leaving the Military™ Transition Strategy

At this point, you should be nearing 50% progress along your transition timeline (across the horizontal axis of this diagram) and you should start to feel pretty good about your plan and where you are headed.

During this timeline review, plan in details such as:

o   timing of terminal leave (or leave prior to final PCS)

o   location of family members throughout the process

o   your location during the transition and preferences for location (if any) once the transition is complete

o   resume completion date

o   mock interviewing timeline: when, where and with whom

o   and more!

As you plan your way through this timeline and add this level of detail, you will be able to better visualize your path for the future and to see yourself completing a successful and fulfilling transition into your new role into corporate America.

You will notice that 70% of the overall timeline is allocated to this point in your transition process. This is for a good reason. At each of the prior steps, you've started on completely new subject areas and included them into your preparation. During this final section of your timeline, you must bring all of the sections together and make them work. Take some time to review each of the areas and continue to refine your delivery to include the example of what to expect on interview day.

Bring together all of the details that we've discussed, such as your interview wardrobe, resume, interviewing skills, and input from your transitioning team. Be sure to review the examples of the common mistakes that military-experienced candidates make when transitioning. From this point on, we will be talking about what to do after the interview, how to properly follow up and how to make a splash in your new role in corporate America.

The point is that now is the time to bring it all together to be ready for your first pairing with corporate America, to successfully complete your first phone or in-person interview.

We talked about a typical onsite interview during Chapter Five. If you are working with a recruiter, they are likely to help you through all of the specifics and travel details to get you onsite and ready to go with the interview. From there, it is up to you to apply what you learned and effectively communicate why you are a good fit for the role, the team and the company.

After the Interview is Over

You will also want to remember to "close" with each of your interviewers by letting them know how interested you are in the role and what a good match you feel you would be with the company (if that is the case). Be sure that you ask for a business card from each of your interviewers to make it easy to follow up with them or to ask questions in the future.

Chapter Five talked about the importance of asking about what to expect after the onsite interview is complete. Most companies will cover this with you, but, as a reminder, don't leave yourself in the dark by not asking if they don't provide the information. Who will call you? If you have questions, who should you call? What is the normal timeline for follow up? What are the next steps for successful candidates? (Etc.)

Once the onsite interview is complete, there are some things that you can do to help to ensure that your rock solid performance will stay fresh on the hiring manager's and team members' minds.

First of all, at the completion of each interview session, you collected business cards with each person's contact information. Use it! In today's world, I recommend submitting these follow-up letters through email and doing it promptly— later that same day or early the following morning directly after the interview. Don't wait too long! The idea is that a letter like this can help to push one interviewer over the fence if there were any questions in his/her mind about you. This may seem like an old fashioned, over rated step to take, but not many candidates are in the habit of doing this today. Listen when I tell you that it is an excellent way to differentiate yourself as a candidate.

Try to personalize each letter. Include detail from your conversation or from your time with that person to help them recall the details. Since you may have been brought in with many other candidates on interview day, it is important that you find every way possible to distinguish yourself and help them to recall your excitement about and fit for the position. Let's look at *an example follow-up letter format.*

Your name

Your address

Your email

Your *verified* cell phone number

Date

Contact name

Company name

Company address

Dear [First Name],

It was great talking with you during my onsite interview yesterday. Thanks for the opportunity to be considered for this exciting position on your team.

I was particularly excited to hear about the team's plan to get back to basics and improve customer satisfaction. I know from the enthusiasm on the team that these efforts will be successful.

I feel very strongly that I will be a great addition to this team. I hope to get the opportunity to use my strong leadership skills and experience to magnify the team's effort to improve customer satisfaction.

Please don't hesitate to contact me at any time. I look forward to talking with you again and to moving forward with my candidacy for this role as a _____ on your team.

Best regards,

firstname lastname

Before sending these letters, be sure to check and double-check your grammar, spelling and punctuation. Absolutely confirm the contact information that you have listed. The hiring manager may only have a few minutes to call and you want to be absolutely certain that you are easy to reach.

Be sure to send this letter to everyone on the team. You may have felt a stronger connection with one team member than another, but if you send this letter to one of the people on the interview team, be sure to send one to everyone (especially to the one who have may doubts about you!).

Reviewing Your Performance

As you review the results of interview day in your head to assess how you did or what to expect, be careful. It can be very hard to tell. Some interviewers naturally have more of a critical or "bad cop" type nature when they are talking with you. Others that seem interested and pleasant may seem to really appreciate everything that you have to say, more like the "good cop" approach. These can be misleading.

Whether you are trying to draw conclusions during interview day or later on after the interview is complete, don't base it on your perceived attitudes or responses from the interviewers. That is not a safe gauge. Think more about the position and whether or not you provided clear and quantifiable examples of how you have contributed in the past. Think about how you described the examples. If you made it easy for the interviewer to be able to picture you attaining a similar level of accomplishments while at their company in this specific team, then you are likely to get a call.

Most interviewers these days are trained to see beyond the social interaction of two people in an interview room and they are looking for specific real-world competency examples that will improve the odds of you being successful with this new team. Do not try to draw conclusions from how they respond verbally or with body language. In many cases, you will be misled.

In fact, I strongly recommend that you don't try to tally your score or to gauge your results at any point during the day. Many successful interviews will give you that feeling in the pit of your stomach that everything is going great, but not all of them. On the flip side, many unsuccessful interviews may seem like they are going fine until you find out that they are no longer interested.

If you go through the interview process with the mental picture of you running an individual race against the clock, where you will only get your final score or finishing results (i.e. feedback on your performance) once your cross the finish line, you will do just fine. Don't try to tally the results as you go along because the team is not attempting to do this either. It is likely that the interview team will not be able to get together until after you've left to talk about how you did. Each new interviewer or interviewing team should be looked at as a fresh start and its own opportunity to "wow" them with your high level of interest and qualification for the open position.

Now what?

So, now that you have completed your telephone (and incredibly successful) onsite interview and you've followed up with the thank-you notes, now what? If you've planned your transition timeline successfully, you may be heading out on additional interviews. This is really the right answer and will also help you to get your mind off of the waiting. For the reasons that are mentioned above, you don't want to put "all of your eggs in one basket." You want to be sure that you've explored a couple of options in corporate America. Multiple interviews can also help you to experience the "ins and outs" of different roles and allow you to experience the culture of the organization during the onsite interview trip.

Just as you did in preparing for your phone interviews, have an area ready to go to receive the phone call with the decision. Have a paper and pen ready to use so that you can take notes during the call.

If they are calling with bad news, remember that it is nothing personal. Interviewing is considered to be more of a science these days with very unforgiving terms. In most cases, you will have to receive across-the-board 100% endorsement in order to be given an offer. A "maybe" is usually considered to be a "no." If you think about this, it is not really a surprise. The company that likes you will make you an offer, train you and teach you about their company, history, their customers and more. They will enroll you in benefits and may relocate you or help with your relocation to your new area. All of this is quite an investment and they want to make sure it is the correct fit on both ends.

I know that with my early interviews, a "no" was something that was hard to take. I had prepared myself and learned about all of the companies and their customers and more. Why weren't they interested? What I now realize is that if the fit is not quite right, it is much better to determine this during the interview than to wait a few months or a few years and to experience the frustration on both sides. I had invested a lot of time and money on my end as well and would continue to invest as we went along the decision-making timeline. You don't want to give up too early, but don't look at an interview that does not result in an offer as a failure.

Not every role or every company was made to match properly with every person. Work to determine this as soon as possible in the employment cycle — during the interview, if possible. If you get a chance to talk with the hiring manager or individual that delivers the bad news to you, ask for feedback. You may receive it. Some companies may not release this for legal concerns, but I recommend that you ask for it. Also, if you are lucky enough to receive it, graciously accept it. Think about how to use it in the future. Now is not the time to defend yourself. If your feedback is that the team did not think that you were aggressive enough to successfully manage the work environment, but you've been a semi-professional wrestler for most of your life, don't get defensive. Think about how your delivery fell through. Think about how you will watch for this type of situation in the future and prevent it by more clearly portraying your competency match.

What if it's a "yes"?

So, what happens if it is a "yes?" Most hiring managers or teams will give you a call directly to give you the good news or at least to give you an idea of the path that they plan to take. The call will go something like this: "Hi, I am calling with some really great news! We'd like to extend you an offer of employment to …" Take some time to celebrate and share in the excitement with the interviewing team at this point. You've both worked very hard to get to the point of having a match on both sides.

Once the party is over, have some specific questions ready to go. They should go over the basics of the offer with you over the phone, but ask when you can expect to receive the offer in writing. It is very hard to digest the contents of the offer while you are still on the phone and you'll want to be sure that nothing is overlooked from either end. Be sure to take notes on all of the benefits that are included and write them down.

If you are not certain what each one of the benefits is, ask. You might feel silly asking about 401K plans or PPOs or HMOs, but don't allow this to influence you. I assure you that new employees at all levels of the organizations will ask the same types of questions. These plans vary from company to company and from location to location, so these types of question are not unique to the person transitioning from the military. Be sure that you are very familiar with the relocation assistance that will be provided to you from the military. You'll want to keep that in mind, as you may have a say on what if any relocation benefits are included. If you are speaking with someone in the hiring group, you may find that all of your benefit-related questions cannot be immediately answered. They may refer you to a professional that can help in the HR (Human Resources) division of the organization.

Continue down this path for each of the onsite interviews that you've completed. Learn from your mistakes and take some time to celebrate your successes. Respect all of the deadlines or expiration dates with each of the offers that you receive. If you feel that you will not be ready to make your decision by the deadline, ask for more time, but be prepared for a "no." Most companies will work with you within reason to adjust your timeline slightly if you are upfront with your timeline and with your plan, but it can be difficult for an employer to hold positions open for you while you try to make up your mind. They may realize that if you are not initially excited enough to give a resounding "yes," then it may not be the best fit after all.

If you have to deal with multiple offers, congratulations! Yes, it will feel stressful at the time, but remember how fortunate you are and how hard you've worked to make it to the place where two companies in corporate America are calling upon you to join their team. However, don't spend too much time reveling in your successes because you've got work to do and likely a tight timeline in which to respond.

Negotiating Multiple Offers

If you get to the point where you've got multiple offers to be considered, you'll want to handle them carefully. Again, if you are working with a recruiter, this is a great time to get them involved, if they are not already. One of the advantages of multiple offers is that it can be used as a negotiating point.

First, you have to determine if more than one of the offers is attractive to you. If so, how do they compare? You should consider the relative value of all of the benefits of the offer package — such as health care, retirement plans, stock plans, relocation and bonuses —to better understand this. If you see a large gap across multiple roles that interest you, summarize the difference between the two offers. Consult with your recruiter, if applicable, for advice here. In many cases, the recruiter will take care of this communication and negotiation for you, but you will want to be the leader of the effort.

If you are working without a recruiter, make a comparison across all of the benefits and contact the hiring manager and ask for some time to talk more about the offer. They are likely to want to hear the details of the competing offer to which you are referring. Share the information along with your desired outcome of the negotiation. At this point in the hiring process, as long as you are professional throughout the process and are genuinely interested in the role, there is no reason not to negotiate.

Professional communication, at this point in the process, means being upfront about your employment goals and sharing all pertinent information openly. It is important to make the time and the effort to talk through this negotiation with the hiring manager in as much detail as he/she would like.

The Leaving the Military™ Transition Decision Matrix

Let's look at a tool from the military staff school and from the Lean Six Sigma Process Improvement Tool Kit that can help you to consider your decision from a mathematical perspective. It is called a Decision Matrix.

Leaving the Military™ Decision Matrix

Positions considered - score values from 1 = low to 10 = high in each area.

Variables Considered	Weighted importance of variables (1% to 100%)	Sales Rep for ABC Corp		Financial Analyst for Serve, Inc		Manufacturing Team Leader	
1. Challenge of position	70%	3	2.1	7	4.9	5	3.5
2. Career path of position	90%	7	6.3	6	5.4	4	3.6
3. Location fit for my spouse's employment	70%	3	2.1	6	4.2	6	4.2
4. Salary	75%	5	3.75	6	4.5	5	3.75
5. Benefits	60%	8	4.8	5	3	6	3.6
6. Skill set to be developed in this position	85%	10	8.5	9	7.65	8	6.8
		Weighted Score	28	Weighted Score	30	Weighted Score	25

This position is the best
match on the identified criteria!

Instructions for Completion

Step 1: Fill in the colored boxes across the top horizontally. Include all positions that you are considering for employment.

Step 2: Fill in the variables that you consider to be important when making this decision. Consult with your family and transitioning team members to be sure that none are missed.

Step 3: Weight each of the variables from a low or not important rating of 0% to a high or very important rating of 100%.

Step 4: Score each of the columns under the positions considered for each of the variables on the left most column. Score them on a scale of 1 as a low rating (or poor match) to 10 as a high rating (or a high match for this variable).

Step 5: Calculate out the cells with spreadsheet functions or using a calculator to determine the weighted value of each position/variable combination. List this value to the right of the 1-10 score for each position.

Step 6: Total the weighted score for all of the variables for the positions in the lowest boxes for each position. This is the weighted total for each position considered. The highest score represents the position with the best match for your given criteria.

Use the Leaving the Military™ Transition Decision Matrix to assist you in your decision-making process. It can be very valuable as you work to juggle around in your head all of the factors that are important to you when making the sometimes complicated decision of which position to accept. Get your thoughts and priorities out on paper and then spend some time discussing this with your family and transition team to find the right answer.

Here is a blank Leaving the Military™ Transition Decision Matrix for you to work with:

Leaving the Military ™ Decision Matrix

Positions considered - score values from 1 = low to 10 = high in each area.

Variables Considered									Weighted Score		Weighted Score		Weighted Score

*Note: Variables considered and weighting must be updated to personal decision criteria. What's important to you?

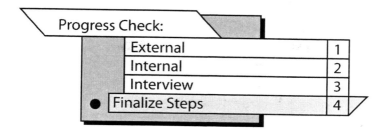

Chapter Six (Interactive)

Get Started! Fight procrastination! Do it now!

1. Describe your goals here for working with or working without a recruiter. _____

_____

_____

_____

2. With what type of recruiter are you looking to work? _____

_____

_____

_____

3. How will you share the workload with the recruiter? What transition preparation areas will you complete? In which areas will you request preparation assistance from your recruiter? _____

_____

_____

_____

4. Who do you know that has used a recruiter in the past that you will ask for their referrals or recommendations? _____

_____

_____

_____

5. List recruiting firms that you plan to contact to discuss potential partnerships and your timeline for this effort. _____

_____

_____

_____

6. Describe your plan to follow up with the interviewing team after completing your onsite interview. _____

_____

_____

_____

_____

7. In case of multiple offers for employment, list the weighted criteria that you will use to rank the opportunities prior to accepting. _____

_____

_____

_____

_____

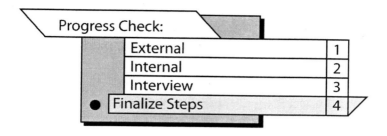

Chapter Seven

Go! Hit the ground running in your new role!

It has been a pretty hectic transition timeline and path for you as you've found your way to corporate America. I can safely say this no matter if you were able to start your preparation two years before transitioning or if it was a two-month project prior to the end of your most recent PCS. With this hectic timeline, you probably have not had a lot of time to think about what the first days would be like or how you would approach them once you've accepted that position.

Congratulations! You are now a member of corporate America!

Preparing For Your New Role and Life as a Civilian

In preparing for your new role and life as a civilian, start by taking a deep breath. You will be happy to know that many of the approaches that you used in your military life to be successful and to accomplish tasks will be successful in the civilian world. If you are ever in doubt, go with what you know!

Let's talk more about this. When I started my first role in corporate America, I was determined to be successful. It was a long time in coming and I had prepared a great deal. I also knew that my employer had paid a healthy amount in recruiting fees and I wanted to make sure that I was able to deliver a healthy return on this investment. I found that, at first, I was torn between being the leader that I knew that I could be and with merely observing to learn more about this new environment.

If you experience the same challenge, I recommend that you go with your gut instinct. I found some instances where it was really better to sit back and observe the situation. I knew that I had the leadership skills to make things happen, but I had never been in this organization with this group and I did not want to come off as too pushy. For team meetings, training sessions and events that had an established rhythm, I spent the first few iterations observing and asking questions to understand the current state. After a few times through the routine, I got involved to provide leadership input to the event and to be an active part of determining the future.

Coming in as the new military experienced hire, I was lucky to also receive the advice from others who had transitioned before. They told me about their frustrations coming in to the organization. They had come to expect a certain level of respect or rank in the military that was no longer present in this new world. They found less structure to the organization and fewer boundaries in who contributed to which groups and who made the decisions. For me, having someone detail their frustration or adjustment made it easier for me to plan for these changes and make the necessary adjustments. Ask for their advice and use what you can.

As I continued in the role, I found other places where I could do less observing and become more of a leader from the start. For any projects or efforts that were new, that had not yet reached a certain rhythm or routine with the group, I added my input from the start. I did not wait to try to understand the current situation, as it did not yet exist. I threw in my input and debated with the group right from the start.

Most employers are looking for something similar in a new employee. They want to know that you are going to be a compassionate leader, that you will step in and lead when needed, but also know when to stand back and learn from the group. This is something to take and apply in your own way, but the bottom line is that the skills that you learned in the military will, for the most part, transfer directly over into your new role in corporate America.

Which skills will transfer directly and which ones will need the most development?

If you are wondering what type of skills will transfer directly and which ones will need the most development, let's look at the following chart.

Leaving the Military™ Kick Start Strategy

Leverage your strengths, Develop your weaknesses!

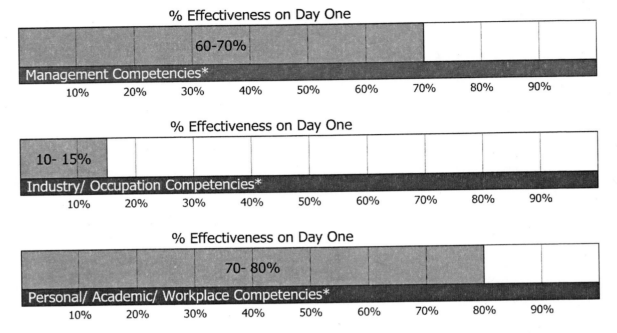

* As split by Department of Labor: www.careeronestop.org/competencymodel/tool_step1.aspx

Keep this picture in the back of your mind as you prepare for day one in your new role in corporate America. It is broken into three categories: management competencies, industry/occupation competencies and personal/academic/workplace competencies. The blue bar that extends from left to right indicates the level of effectiveness that you have in each of these areas. A blank diagram is provided on the next page for you to fill in on your own later. This diagram represents my experience with many military candidates transitioning into an initial role in corporate America. Keep in mind that this tool or graphic outline is new, but, again, the competency definitions and groupings can be seen on the Department of Labor website mentioned above.

How can I generalize like this? In the military, all individuals received a fair-to-extensive amount of leadership or management training in areas such as developing your team, motivating your peers and your team, decision making, risk analysis, general leadership and planning. This is not the case for training programs in the civilian world.

In the military, you were trained how to lead and manage people by being put in charge of a group from day one, whether it was a training exercise, a section of your unit, or a cross-functional maintenance team working to complete a task. Without getting into a debate on what is leadership and what is management, let's look at the corporate side. Your peers in the civilian world are not exposed to this type of environment until it is time to lead, some number of years later in their career when it has been determined that they are ready.

This is a huge advantage to you as you start off that should bring you a good amount of confidence in what you are doing. It is also portrayed on the diagram with the first horizontal blue bar extending to the 60- 70% position from left to right. It is an inherent strength!

The second horizontal bar is labeled "Industry/Occupation Competencies" and is only given a value of 10-15%. This is because a transition from the military to corporate America is considered a career transition. Where you may have worked on repairing missile launchers in the military, you may now be preparing marketing strategies and events. In this example, your leadership skills (as discussed earlier) will still be applicable, but your industry and occupation competencies will have to be significantly adjusted.

The third horizontal bar is labeled "Personal/Academic/Workplace Competencies. I've rated this bar as, generally, highest of all. Most military candidates find that their education and workplace skills transfer very well into corporate America as they have a higher than average amount of education and have learned to work with all types of people on all types of projects to yield excellent results.

Take this blank chart and personalize it with your own level of experience and your role in corporate America. This is a rough estimate, so don't get too caught up on it. Update the values and then work to plan your approach.

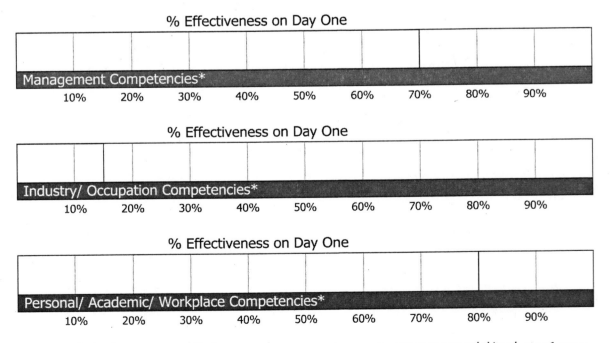

Leaving the Military™ Kick Start Strategy

Leverage your strengths, Develop your weaknesses!

% Effectiveness on Day One

Management Competencies*

10% 20% 30% 40% 50% 60% 70% 80% 90%

% Effectiveness on Day One

Industry/ Occupation Competencies*

10% 20% 30% 40% 50% 60% 70% 80% 90%

% Effectiveness on Day One

Personal/ Academic/ Workplace Competencies*

10% 20% 30% 40% 50% 60% 70% 80% 90%

* As split by Department of Labor: www.careeronestop.org/competencymodel/tool_step1.aspx

In order to help with your efforts to complete this chart, let's talk more about each area, while keeping it simple.

Completing the Chart

Look at "Management Competencies." This category refers to your ability to lead and to manage at all levels in the organization. Think about how you motivate your peers and your team in the military to internalize or develop goals and how you keep them on track to meet or to exceed them. Now, think about what you know about your new role. It is possible that your experience at this point in the organization may be limited, but it is enough to get you started.

Is this new environment similar to one of your past military environments? If so, will you be able to operate as you have in the past, without much modification? ***Picture your previous work experience in the military and then picture applying the same approach in your new role and environment.*** How much of an adjustment do you expect will be needed? You are likely to end up somewhere near the above estimate with 70% carrying over directly, but make your own estimate.

If, as you are going through this exercise, you find that you would like more information on these competencies or their split, visit the Department of Labor website, as you did earlier, for help: http://www.careeronestop.org/CompetencyModel/. Also, remember to keep the end result in mind. You don't need to be an expert in competency models or definitions.

Spend as little time as possible wondering if you are on the correct path to be successful. Consider your performance risk in making this transition. Familiar work environments or roles carry little risk if you've performed well in them in the past. Unfamiliar work environments should be considered uncharted territory and handled more carefully.

The goal in this chapter is to make you comfortable in your first days in the role by establishing your strengths and planning for your weaknesses, so let's continue.

Look at "Industry/Occupation Competencies" and think about where you've been in the military. In what type of industry did you spend the most of your time? How does this compare with where you're headed in corporate America? What type of occupational experience did you gain in the military and how does it compare with corporate America? If you spent time in the military fixing or managing maintenance with aircraft and now you are heading to corporate America to lead a team of maintenance-focused service professionals, you'll probably see a good amount of overlap. If you were a pilot in the Air Force and now you'll be writing technical documents, you will probably have less of an overlap in experience. Plan for it.

Look at the "Personal/Academic/Workplace" bar and make the same estimate. If all of the areas are too much, focus on one or two to develop a plan. Think of "personal" as the manner in which you work: your personal level of discipline and work environment preferences from the past. Match your academic achievements with the workplace. Are you an engineer who will be heading in to a technical design role or into a marketing role? Have you spent all of your time in the military workplace and now you'll be part of a distributed work environment working remotely? All of these scenarios require a different amount of adjustment.

What to Do in Areas That Match and Those That Don't

Now that you've sketched in each bar and have a good idea of what skills or competency areas will match and which will require a greater adjustment, be aware of these areas and plan for them. With the areas that match, plan to operate much as you did in the past with little adjustment. If you planned maintenance support for your military customer units and now you will be scheduling and communicating maintenance support across customer locations, a lot of familiar situations will present themselves. You will be able to act off of your experience with confidence.

In this type of situation, where you've done something or worked in a very similar environment, you will notice this by having a feeling of familiarity. You will also sense the right approach and the first steps to take to get started. Go with it! The number one takeaway from this chapter should be that when things look and feel familiar, and you aren't sure if you should act, do it! Initiative is a valued skill in the military just as much as — if not more so — in the civilian world. If you have the idea of what to do and need the confirmation, develop the plan and take it to a peer or to your manager for review. Just don't sit back and wait. ***Avoid hesitation and doubt and put your military skills to work from the start. Take initiative and lead the effort when the opportunity arises.*** Doing this over your first three to six months will allow you to set yourself on the course to being a star performer early in your new civilian career.

If you worked in the criminal investigation division of the military and know you will be planning marketing events for small corporations, you may find some areas that don't match up very well. How should you approach them? For one, you've never worked in a marketing department. The industry and occupation are new to you. Be aware of this and spend some time observing to learn what's new and what the difference is. In this situation, initiative is also a very valuable skill, but you may want to apply it differently. Taking the lead and tackling a problem without hesitation is a great place to start, but you may want to plan more peer or leadership review sessions to be sure that you are on the right track. Just as with any new projects, ask about what's happened in that area before and with what results. Use what worked well and learn from other people's failures. The point is to take the initiative, where possible in both situations, but reduce risk in the more unknown areas by getting more feedback and input along the way.

How to Adjust to Your New Role

In this last example or at some point in your new role, you are likely to look around and wonder how you got into the new situation. At least early on in the role, many things (or, in some cases, too many) may seem to be different. In order to keep yourself on track and confident during this time, remember a few things:

- o You've experienced many transitions in the military. From the beginning of your initial days as a member of the military to a transition to a role of greater authority, you've done this before and been successful. Be confident!

- o The human resources professionals that put you into this role knew what they were doing as they do it every day. If you did not share overwhelming results and proof of your fit for the role, you would not have been hired.

- o This is a career transition and it will take work and focus on your part to be successful in it. Keep your head up and focused on the task and soon it will seem like second nature.

- o Don't avoid problems. Identify them as early as possible. Make them known, gather insight and input from those around you, and solve them.

- o Watch for and avoid being a "busy" person. "Busy" are easy to recognize as they announce this quality to (usually) everyone. They also seem to take a certain amount of pride in the quality, as if being busy was related to delivering results. In general, these people choose to spend most of the time being overscheduled and overwhelmed. Make a conscious decision every day to fit in what is the most important. Don't be the victim of your email inbox or only respond to the loudest request. ***Work on what***

matters the most and do it first. Review your results at the end of the day, the week, and the month to be sure you are working on your priority items first. Consider and use the "Pareto Principle" to keep you on track. The "Pareto Principle" is a term rooted in the early 2oth century that says that 80% of the results are achieved by working on the top 20% of priorities. It helps us when we look for a strategy to prioritize our time, resources or assets. Keep in mind, or find a way to plot the data showing the top 20% (in frequency, cost or other customer-facing variable) and then rightfully focus your efforts there for the greatest result.

o   Have fun and make things fun for your team. Not all successful people know how to do this, but successful and happy people have figured it out! Smiling is a great place to start. It is difficult to be disliked when you are a happy and sincere person.

o   Focus on making other people look good (rather than yourself), especially your team members or subordinates. It takes a self-confident leader to realize this. As a group, you will accomplish more together in this environment, your team members will be happier and your recognition will come naturally.

o   If, for some reason, your new team does not have a review program (not likely) or a plan for you to get regular feedback from your team and your manager, be sure to ask for one. Make sure you are always given ideas for improvement. Don't let anyone get away with telling you that you are doing "great." Ask for *specifics* on what is going well and what needs improvement.

- o It is normal to have moments of doubt as you go through your first few months or year. Recognize this for what it is — a normal outcome of a career transition. However, if the moments of doubt start to turn into dissatisfaction, do something about it. Talk to your manager or peers. (Refer to the Appendix E, "Help, this is not what I expected!", for more ideas.)

- o Remember to **focus on customers**, both internal and external. Tell them that you consider them customers and that their level of satisfaction is very important to you. Ask them how you can make their job or life easier and ask for regular feedback on your performance. Always work to increase your customers' level of satisfaction.

You've now built the vision for being an initiative-driven leader in your new role who is aware of which areas will require more input in order for you to be sure of your success. You also know which areas are likely to carry over very well from the military with little adjustment and little supervision.

Congratulations on all of your hard work to get to this point. Be sure to thank your transition team for their help in getting you to this point — prepared to take the reins of your successful career in corporate America! Also, take some time to celebrate. You, your family and your transition team have all worked hard to get you to this point. Recognize and celebrate this accomplishment.

Get started and good luck!

Chapter Seven (Interactive)

Get Started! Fight procrastination! Do it now!

1. Complete your Leaving the Military™ Kick Start Strategy diagram and summarize the results here. Which competency groups will carry over with little adjustment? Which ones will not?

_____

_____

_____

_____

_____

2. List specific work examples that match well with your current role. Plan how you will use this match. _____

_____

_____

_____

_____

_____

_____

3. List specific areas in your current role that will be new to you. Plan what you will do to be successful with them. _____

_____

_____

_____

_____

4. Write out your plan to take initiative in your new role over the first few months.

_____

_____

_____

_____

_____

5. Discuss how you will apply and how you will use the Pareto Principle (the "80/20" rule) to keep yourself on track to work on the most important items first.

_____

_____

_____

_____

Appendix A

Suggested Reading List — Some Great Places to Start!

o *Good to Great: Why Some Companies Make the Leap... and Others Don't* by Jim Collins. This is a great book with data on what makes companies successful.

o *How to Win Friends and Influence People* by Dale Carnegie. This book is a classic on how the little things matter.

o *The 7 Habits of Highly Effective People* by Stephen R. Covey. This classic gives great insight into successful habits.

o *Execution: The Discipline of Getting Things Done* by Larry Bossidy and Ram Charan. This is a great book on how successful people get things done.

o *The Toyota Way* by Jeffrey Liker. This is a great book on quality, lean production and process improvement by the world's #1 auto maker.

o *301 Smart Answers to Tough Interview Questions* by Vicky Oliver. This book will help you to prepare and polish your delivery for interview day.

o *Achieve Sales Excellence: The 7 Customer Rules for Becoming the New Sales Professional* by Howard Stevens and Theodore Kinni. This book will give you more background on the successful sales approach of consulting with customers to determine and fill their needs.

o ***Who says elephants can't dance? Inside IBM's Historic Turn Around*** by Louis Gerstner, Jr. This book details a great example of re-making a corporation.

o ***The 21 Irrefutable Laws of Leadership: Follow Them and People Will Follow You*** by John C. Maxwell. John Maxwell's books give great leadership insight.

o ***The Art of Closing the Sale: The Key to Making More Money Faster in the World of Professional Selling*** by Brian Tracy. This book will further refine the sales approach offered in Achieve Sales Excellence, with focus placed on closing the deal.

Appendix B

Some Good Reasons To Consider

Not Leaving the Military Before Retirement

- o **Job Security:** Yes, the military goes through ups and downs in its recruiting cycle, but it is a relatively stable environment. The cyclical nature of the military is less erratic than that of corporate America. As we discussed earlier, the only group that guarantees job security in corporate America is the customer and many forces exist that can affect customer satisfaction. Anything from government regulations to emerging technology can make your division or your company — and, therefore, your employment status — uncertain.

- o **Benefits:** You may have heard on the news about huge executive or CEO retirement or compensation packages. The news is covered with stories of stock compensated millionaires and the like. These things certainly do happen, but not to everyone. In fact, as this is considered a career transition by corporate America, you are likely to experience a cut in pay and benefits for at least the short term after leaving the military. For example, in many cases, you are likely to start off with two weeks vacation at the start of your new career. If you like to move with your job, you may be disappointed with corporate America. It just does not make good business sense for most companies to move you with all of your possessions and family members every few years.

On the flip side of all of this, many people are likely to enjoy the idea of compensation based on performance. In corporate America, everyone does not progress together based on time on the job. It is a meritocracy, with high performers advancing more rapidly and being compensated at a higher level.

- **Tax Advantages:** Many of the tax incentives that you experience in the military will not carry over to corporate America. Military members are able to take advantage of their home state's income tax rate. For some people, this means no income tax for the duration of their time in the military, no matter the location. This flexibility does not exist in the civilian world. Tax relief on deployment income, or on items such as food purchased at the commissary or on housing allowances are also not likely to be found in corporate America.

- **Camaraderie and Team Cohesion:** This is not to say that you won't find yourself as the part of a tight-knit group in your new role in corporate America.

A lot of high-functioning, productive and really fun teams exist out there today, but they will never be the same as what you experienced in the military. Part of this stems from being taken off of the 24/7 mentality, where you and your military team have worked together in all parts of the world, at all times of the day and night in all kinds of conditions. Another part of this stems from the fact that in the military, team members' lives depend on and their ability to work with and trust each other.

Some transitioning military members have been frustrated or disappointed by this area. The lack of constant communication and "tie-in" with the team and its goals can be taken as a sign of an unmotivated team or an undedicated environment. Of course, this is not likely to be the case, but it certainly is a different environment in corporate America than in the military.

On the flip side of this, it is great to have the option of turning off your cell phone on the weekend and not having to worry about being on-call continuously at all hours of the day and night. Also, you may find it convenient to not be overwhelmed with the workload or work schedule of even the most demanding teams in corporate America.

o **Early Retirement and Pension Benefits**: The military retirement can be a great path to a second career at a relatively young age. In fact, not many companies in corporate America offer any kind of pension package or guaranteed benefits and health care at the age of full retirement. Some that do today are debating and reviewing changes for tomorrow with no guaranteed coverage.

For this reason, a military retirement can be a wonderful thing, with guaranteed income and guaranteed healthcare. This is especially true in today's healthcare environment with millions of uninsured patients and skyrocketing healthcare costs.

o **Healthy Lifestyle**: The branches of the military promote a healthy lifestyle, with many of them planning time for physical activity into the work day. Although many corporations offer gym memberships or access to onsite gyms as an incentive, it is up to the employees to find the time to fit this activity into your daily routine.

Appendix C

"Leaning Forward in Your Foxhole"

Proactively addressing the common weaknesses of the military experienced candidate entering corporate America.

With similarities across the military branches' on-boarding and missions, a parallel can be seen across the majority of military candidates looking to transition to corporate America. Focus on these areas, listed in priority order, and their development in order to further stand out in the crowd:

- **Business Acumen**: This is your knowledge of and ability to understand and communicate the financial side of corporate America. In order to improve in this area, look for and read books that will introduce you to the world of finance and accounting. Be sure to understand the basics such as: income statements, profit and loss statements, and balance sheets. Take a course to help you to learn about these concepts and to be able to discuss them in a group setting. Read potential future employer's annual reports, focusing on the first 10% of the report and on the financial data with notes. Develop a study group to learn and discuss these terms and concepts as a group.

- **Communication Skills**: Practice talking without all of the complicated military jargon and acronyms. Learn to talk in a way that your new company and team will understand. If in doubt, talk as if you were describing a role or a situation as you would to a non-military-experienced family member to keep yourself within boundaries.

o **Walk, talk and think with a customer focus!** Remember, the only job security in corporate America comes from customer satisfaction. Think about what external and internal customers expect from you in your new/future role. Find a way to get internal and external feedback on your ability to meet or exceed their goals. Competitively focus on improving your performance level!

o **Learn about sales** even if it is not your desired career path. A sales organization and mindset are at the heart of all successful corporations. Good employees understand that sales define the success of the entire organizations and that they must be empowered to be successful and to exceed customer expectations. It is also very important to understand "consultative sales."

If the word "sales" brings to mind the typical pushy used car salesperson, then start reading — you've got a lot to learn. The bottom line is that a successful "consultative" sale is a result of determining a customer's needs and then developing and communicating a solution to their problem. The only pressure that should ever be felt is on the part of the customer after they have seen or heard the solution and know that what you are selling is something that they must have in order to solve their problem or to increase their own customers' satisfaction. Look for and read a book on "consultative selling" to better understand successful sales today.

o Research and develop a basic understanding of one of the forms of **quality management or process improvement**. Learn to understand why quality and continuous improvement must be on the minds of all employees in order for your new company to survive or to prosper in today's competitive global environment. Research one technique (Lean Process Improvement, Total Quality Management [TQM], The Eight Disciplines [8D], Six Sigma or other) and make it a part of the way that you operate.

o **Business Ethics and Integrity**: Of course ethics and integrity are nothing new to you as you leave the military, but research some of the terrible downturns of the last decade to understand why it is such a hot topic today in corporate America. Fiascos such as the collapse of Enron have scarred and horrified families, governments and corporations and exemplify the need to constantly re-voice the importance of ethics and integrity in a corporate environment.

Appendix D

Helpful Tips for the Transitioning Military Spouse

Kudos to the military spouse, supportive from the start, "holding down the fort" at a moment's notice and always asked to do more. For him or her, it can be difficult to visualize the right role during this time of transition. A little more information in your corner can be very beneficial to the entire family, as you can assume the leadership role that you've taken on in the past to help lead the family through yet-another transition. Here are some suggestions to get involved and to help to keep everyone on track:

- **Be as supportive and involved** as you have in the past. As many spouses struggle to balance their career with their military spouses or even plan for gaps in their career for the benefit of the family, an active role in this transition can benefit both of you. Your spouse really could use help at this point to make sure that the hands-on practice in the form of mock interviews and dress rehearsals happens.

  If you, yourself will consider picking up your career at this new location, or somewhere later on down the road, practice with resume writing and interview preparation can really help you to stay on top of these depleting skills.

- **The "Open to Location" Decision**: One of the many attractive points to hiring military candidates is that many of them are flexible on location and may actually enjoy moving from time to time. It can be very difficult for corporate America to match candidate preferences with available locations without some level of flexibility. Remove as many limiters from your spouse's candidacy by being as flexible as possible on location. Also, with the last change of station leaving the military being covered by the military, many military hiring programs are promoted to corporate America based on these savings.

My advice here is to encourage you both to be as open as possible on location in order to be able to find the best "fit" in corporate America. It is also very important to be realistic. If you know that you and the family will be miserable in a certain location after spending time researching it, don't go there. In the long run, it would turn out poorly for the entire family.

- o **Keep your options open and get involved in the selection process.** Early on in the transition process may be too early to voice preferences on locations as an employer may not be certain on all open locations. Also, an interviewing employer is likely to wonder about the priorities of a candidate if the first question out of his/her mouth is about location or opportunities in the area for spouse employment. Try to help your spouse to focus early on in the process on proving their fit for the positions that match with transitioning goals. Save the detailed discussions on location and benefits for after your spouse has proven his/her fit and has received an offer or multiple offers for employment.

However, once you make it to the point where your spouse (hopefully) has multiple offers to consider, get involved and voice your preferences. Include your preferences for employment options or location in your "transition decision matrix" to find the best choice for the whole family.

Appendix E

"Help! This is not what I expected (or signed up for)!"

(What to do when it doesn't seem to be working out.)

On occasion, but luckily at a relatively low rate, a military-experienced hire (or any recently hired employee, for that matter) will find themselves in a work environment that is not what they expected. The transition from the military to corporate America is not so simple. Your preparation through this outline helped to reduce the odds of this happening greatly, but not completely.

How do you know if you are in this situation? This feeling is based on more than just a temporary situation. It is not based on frustration with one project or with one team member, but more of a trend that starts to develop and grow over time. (By the way, I would not try to draw any conclusions about this until an ample amount of time on the job — at least three to six months.) This situation will show its face by a loss of productivity and impact along with at the same time a drastic increase in frustration.

If you start to see this happening regularly, it is important not to try to "look the other way." It is also important not to overreact. Conduct some deep soul-searching.

It is important to clear up any confusion as early as possible. Think clearly about what you expected when you came into the role and what you are now experiencing and communicate it with your manager. Do this as early as possible and try to phrase it in a positive way, but be clear.

If, for some reason, you are not comfortable talking with your manager, go to the human resources department and make an appointment to talk with them. Try to be as clear and well thought out as possible when summarizing your concerns. You may also want to go talk with other military-experienced workers in the company to talk with them. They may be able to help you to get through this difficult time.

In the end, remember that if you are truly not happy and did not come into the role or environment that you expected, then you are not performing up to your capability and the situation is a losing one for both you and your employer. In this situation, it may be better to part ways amicably knowing that each one of you will be able to learn from the mismatch and find a better pairing with someone else. It is important to remember to avoid making this a personal situation. There may be frustration and disappointment on both ends, but keep it at a professional level.

Appendix F

A Summary of the Author-Developed Tools and Visuals

I. Leaving the Military™ Transition Strategy Diagram. Use this diagram to plan and to stay on track throughout your transition timeline.

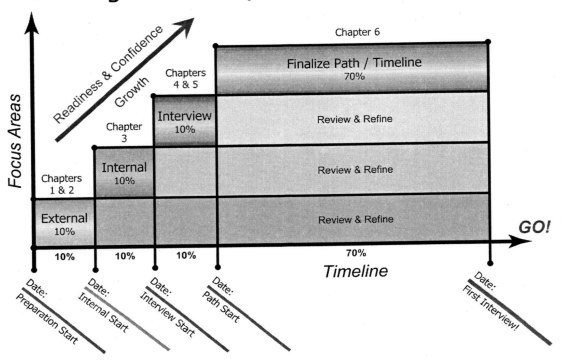

II. Leaving the Military™ Perceived Performance Curve: Apply linear effort to your goals, but expect plateaus and growth spurts. Consider the plateaus and perceived set backs as the doors to the breakthrough points that will bring your greatest accomplishments and results!

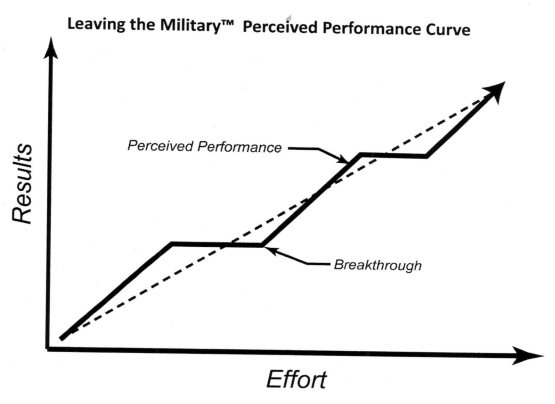

Leaving the Military™ Perceived Performance Curve

III. Leaving the Military™ Competency Matrix: Use this tool to match your accomplishments with your competency profile/strengths. Later, map the positions that you are considering into your accomplishment listing. The ranked results will help to better prepare you for interview day. This tool can also be used to customize a resume and interview examples for a specific position.

Leaving the Military™ Interviewing Preparation Competency Matrix:							
Name: _____							
Date: _____							

Step 1: Complete accomplishment/ competency match.

1b. List competencies displayed here:

1a. List accomplishments here:	a.	b.	c.	d.	e.	f.
1.						
2.						
3.						
4						
5						
6						
7						
8						

1c. Place a " ☆ " at the intersection of an accomplishment/ competency match.

Step 2: Complete accomplishment/ competency match for desired positions.

2b. Copy competency list from above:

2a. List desired positions here:	a.	b.	c.	d.	e.	f.
1.						
2.						
3.						
4.						
5.						
6.						
7.						
8.						

2c. Place a " ☆ " at the intersection of a desired position/ competency needed match.

IV. Leaving the Military™ Transition Decision Matrix: Use this tool to assist by mathematically portraying the difference between multiple attractive and competing offers.

Leaving the Military ™ Decision Matrix

Positions considered - score values from 1 = low to 10 = high in each area.

Variables Considered				Weighted Score		Weighted Score		Weighted Score	

*Note: Variables considered and weighting must be updated to personal decision criteria. What's important to you?

V. The Leaving the Military™ Kick Start Strategy Diagram: Use this

diagram to summarize and plan for your strengths and weaknesses coming in to

your new role in corporate America.

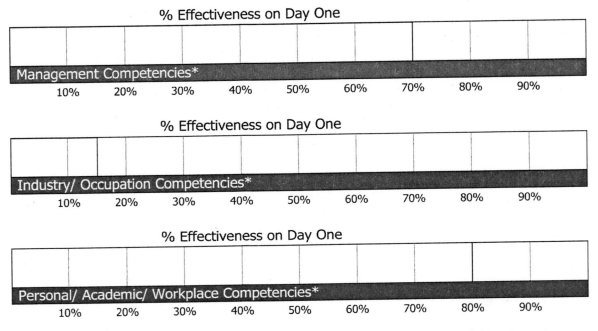

Leaving the Military™ Kick Start Strategy

Leverage your strengths, Develop your weaknesses!

% Effectiveness on Day One

Management Competencies*

10%   20%   30%   40%   50%   60%   70%   80%   90%

% Effectiveness on Day One

Industry/ Occupation Competencies*

10%   20%   30%   40%   50%   60%   70%   80%   90%

% Effectiveness on Day One

Personal/ Academic/ Workplace Competencies*

10%   20%   30%   40%   50%   60%   70%   80%   90%

* As split by Department of Labor: www.careeronestop.org/competencymodel/tool_step1.aspx

Appendix G

What's next?

As you start to settle into your new company, your new home and your new role, you will naturally start to think of the future. This is likely to take months, if not years, but don't be surprised when it does. If you've started the proactive conversations with your manager and your team, this will be an easier topic to consider. During the conversations with your manager, you are likely to cover items very familiar to any After-Action Reviews (AARs) that you completed in the military. You'll go over:

- o what went well

- o what went poorly

- o what you'll plan to do differently next time and how to make that happen

During this conversation, it is a natural to start talking about career progression. Where are you headed in the organization? What are your long-term goals? What are you passionate about or excited to do in the future? These questions probably sound very familiar from your interviewing days, but (thank goodness!) the environment will be very different from the interview environment.

In this case, take advantage of the opportunity with your manager to talk in open dialogue about what's going well, what needs to be improved and where you are headed. Ask for input from your manager and talk about your options for the future. Talk about where other people have gone in the organization from the role that you fill. Explore your options and prioritize your preferences just as you did in the military. Once you set up this plan, vocalize it. Let people in the organization know what your goals are and ask for their advice and input on how to get there. Continue to build your network internally to help to ensure your success.

This is a great time to start thinking more about your long-term goals, something similar to a five-year plan. What type of roles in the organization and in your life are you looking to take on? Where do you want to be professionally and personally? What steps will you need to take to accomplish them. Also, think about what you've done over the last few weeks, months or years, professionally and personally. What went well? What could have gone better? What will you do differently next time? Now, how will you help others coming down your same path to do it better and more efficiently? Ever thought of writing a book?

Congratulations, you've completed the Leaving the Military™

transition process! The best of luck to you in your new world!

Please send your comments, success stories or ideas for improvement to **Marcea@leavingthemilitary.com**. Also, register online at www.leavingthemilitary.com for electronic templates and additional resources to help you as you complete your transition and plan for the future.

Index